This Book is Presented to

_____

By

_____

On the Date of

_____

JIM AMMERMAN
IN HIS OWN WORDS

JIM AMMERMAN
IN HIS OWN WORDS

FOREWORD BY
VERNA LINZEY, D.D.

EDITED BY
GORDON J. KLINGENSCHMITT, PH.D.

MILITARY BIBLE ASSOCIATION
ESCONDIDO, CALIFORNIA

JIM AMMERMAN

In His Own Words

Foreword by
Verna M. Linzey, D.D.

Edited by
Gordon James Klingenschmitt

Copyright © 2012 James F. Linzey
All rights reserved under International Copyright Conventions
All contents used by permission.

Printed in the United States of America

Use of released U.S. Navy and U.S. Department of Defense imagery does not constitute product or organizational endorsement of any kind by the U.S. Navy or the U.S. Department of Defense

Photo of Jim Ammerman: Courtesy of Jim Johnson

ISBNs: 978-1936857-05-0 - Hardcover with Jacket
978-1936857-10-4 - Perfectbound

Library of Congress Control Number: 2011945080

All rights reserved. No part of this book may be reproduced in any form without the permission of the copyright holder. The views expressed in this book are not ¬necessarily those of the publisher nor the editor.

Unless otherwise indicated, Bible quotations are taken from the
Modern English Version

Published by Military Bible Association
Escondido, California, USA

Cover design by Keith Locke

Acknowledgement

I would like to thank Susan Milne for transcribing the interview and making this a high priority. Her attention to detail was of paramount importance and professional. I would like to thank Jim Linzey for not only accepting Jim Ammerman's invitation to conduct the interview, but for conducting it very graciously, providing much needed liberty for Colonel Ammerman to speak freely.

Gordon J. Klingenschmitt, Ph.D.
May 2012

CHAPLAIN (COL) JIM AMMERMAN, USA (RET.)

The event above was the Commencement Ceremony conducted by Kingsway Theological Seminary for the conferral of the Doctor of Divinity degree on Dr. Verna Linzey. Above, Dr. Ammerman reads letters from Lt. Col. Oliver North and Dr. Robert Schuller congratulating Dr. Linzey at this occasion. The event was at the Neighborhood Church Assembly of God in Escondido, California, April 29, 2001. (Photo: courtesy of Jim Johnson)

About Jim Ammerman

E.H. (Jim) Ammerman was the Founding President and Director of Chaplaincy of Full Gospel Churches, Inc. (CFGC). Chaplaincy of Full Gospel Churches is an endorsing agency that is recognized by the Department. of Defense. It is a worldwide ministry that operates from Dallas, Texas, providing support to the U.S. Armed Forces, U.S. Government agencies, and civilian organizations.

Born in Conway, Missouri, on July 20, 1925, Jim is a graduate of Baptist colleges and seminaries. Spirit-filled in 1938, he has been an ordained minister since 1946. He holds a Doctor of Theology degree and a Doctor of Divinity degree.

Jim retired from the U.S. Army in 1977 as a Colonel, having served as an Army chaplain for twenty-three years. During his Army career, Jim served as a paratrooper chaplain with the 82nd Airborne Division and the 101st Airborne Division (while General Westmoreland was commanding) and with the Green Berets for five years. He also served twice with the 1st Cavalry Division and once with the 1st Armor Division. Prior to his service as an Army chaplain, Jim served three and a half years with the Navy as an enlisted radioman and later as a Naval aviator during World War II.

His last European assignment was with V Corps in Frankfurt, Germany, where he supervised eighty-three chaplains representing fourteen denominations who provided religious coverage and support to fifty thousand soldiers and their family members. Jim's last active duty assignment was at Fort Leavenworth, Kansas, where he served as Post Chaplain and pastor to the Command and General Staff College (CGSC). At that time, CGSC annually trained one thousand mid-career officers from the Army and sister services. The graduates of this prestigious school go on to serve as senior leaders of our nation's military, becoming Colonels and Flag Officers.

With literary credits in several professional journals and religious publications, and the books *After the Storm* and *Supernatural Events in the Life of an Ordinary Man*, Jim has appeared frequently on radio and television. Appearances include being a guest on CBN's *700 Club*, *Rays of Hope*, and *Festival of Praise*, and TBN. Additionally, he is a much-loved speaker at Spirit-filled conferences and conventions, including Full Gospel Businessmen's Fellowship International.

COMMENTS

"If it were not for Jim Ammerman I would not have be allowed to remain in the Army as a Chaplain, would not have had the opportunity to be selected and attend the Army War College and would not have had a career of over thirty years of service to our nation. I was a United Methodist Chaplain but felt God leading me on a different path than the UMC was going. I had been filled with the Holy Spirit and God was leading me out of the UMC. As a result, I lost my endorsement and unless I could get another one I would have had to leave the military as a chaplain. At that time there was a small, fairly new, endorsing agency called Chaplaincy of Full Gospel Churches (CFGC) led by Jim Ammerman. After visiting with me he agreed to endorse me and I was allowed to remain in the military as a chaplain. While at a CFGC meeting one night, the U.S. began its attack on Iraq and Desert Storm had begun. Jim Ammerman, my wife, myself and others gathered in a hotel room and prayed for a quick, decisive victory and for protection of the men and women going into combat. Our prayers were answered. I will never forget Jim's faith at the time and will always be thankful for his leadership, friendship and help in my career. God bless you Jim."

CHAPLAIN (COLONEL) ROB NOLAND, USAR (RET.)
FORMER DEPUTY COMMAND CHAPLAIN,
UNITED STATES ARMY RESERVE COMMAND

"I spent two weeks with Jim when we were invited to Ukraine in early 1993 to explore an opportunity to minister to the Ukrainian military forces under the command of General Zoblotny in western Ukraine. For two weeks we traveled together, ministered together and sometimes had to endure conditions that rivaled the Great Depression (which we both survived). There was never a dull moment with Jim. He regaled me with numerous stories of his life and ministry. I never tired of listening…even to the ones he repeated. During the two weeks in Ukraine we formed a bond that has continued for eighteen years as has the ministry we inaugurated together. Jim, I love, respect and appreciate you and your darling Charlene."

COMMANDER, R. GLENN BROWN, CHC, USN (RET.)

"Jim Ammerman served as a watchman of America, seeking not only to preserve the political but especially the spiritual heritage of this great nation. In this book, he tells the story of his life, of God calling him to the ministry through the military, and of the open doors God gave him to equip others desiring to serve as military chaplains. Chaplain Ammerman faithfully served his nation through his military service and he helped preserve the spiritual pillars of America by training thousands of other chaplains to enter the ranks after him. He dedicated his life to God and to his country and he knew the importance of making sure that our nation remembered its true Godly foundations. He not only reflected General George Washington's personal motto, 'For God and My Country,' but he also thoroughly fulfilled one of General Washington's earliest orders to his troops, requiring that "every officer and man will endeavor so to live and act as becomes a Christian soldier, defending the dearest rights and liberties of his country." Col Ammerman did both. A highly influential man of God who not only had great favor with those in authority but who was also a true hero, here is *Jim Ammerman in His Own Words*."

DAVID BARTON
PRESIDENT, WALLBUILDERS

"Colonel Jim Ammerman was a great friend, a great American and a great Christian leader. He and his faithful wife Charlene have been an inspiration to me and to untold thousands by their life and vision for the Chaplaincy of Full Gospel Churches. I always considered it a tremendous honor to fellowship with him and hear his stories of faith. Several times I had the privilege of being a speaker at conferences with him, and those times I will always cherish as his words were pinned to my chest. Though he is now stationed in Heaven, Colonel Jim Ammerman's work continues. I can still hear his voice, challenging us to new heights of faith and courage for the days ahead, similar to when General George Washington desperately needed more troops, Connecticut Governor Jonathan Trumbull sent out an appeal for recruits, August of 1776: 'In this day of calamity, to trust altogether to the justice of our cause, without our utmost exertion, would be tempting Providence....March on! This shall be your warrant: Play the man for God, and for the cities of our God. May the Lord of Hosts, the God of the armies of Israel, be your Captain, your Leader, your Conductor, and Saviour.' "

WILLIAM FEDERER

"As I look back on his life, Jim Ammerman was a patriot who loved America. I was privileged to meet him and to have known him. I wish his family Godspeed in all they attempt to do to honor Jim's legacy, which is the intent of this book."

STANLEY MONTEITH, PH.D.
HOST, RADIO LIBERTY

"*Jim Ammerman In His Own Words* tells the story of a man who successfully opposed religious discrimination against Pentecostal and Charismatic military chaplains. Dr. Ammerman's message in this book eloquently portrays how God used him to cause the Pentagon to take the constitutional rights of military chaplains seriously. I highly recommend it."

JAMES F. LINZEY, D.D.
CHAPLAIN (MAJOR), ARNG (RET.)
PRESIDENT, MILITARY BIBLE ASSOCIATION

"Dr. Jim Ammerman has proven once again that he was a great man of God. He weaves the story of his life as an Army Chaplain and the founding of Chaplaincy of Full Gospel Churches in such a way that it is hard to put the book down once you begin reading it. You will be challenged and stirred as you read the history of such a great man. It is a must read."

WILLIAM OWENS, PH.D.
PRESIDENT, COALITION OF AFRICAN AMERICAN PASTORS
CIVIL RIGHTS ACTIVIST

"Jim Ammerman speaks to the human condition and dire need for divine intervention. He poignantly illustrates how essential it is for believers to follow the edicts of God as witnesses of Christ, despite the onslaught of external pressures. *Jim Ammerman In His Own Words* is a 'must read' for every believer and definitely recommended to all in leadership."

JANICE HOLLIS, PH.D.
FORMER CANDIDATE, LIEUTENANT GOVERNOR, STATE OF PENNSYLVANIA

"Colonel E.H. Jim Ammerman is one of the outstanding "movers and shakers" of the late twentieth and early twenty-first centuries. Quietly and in his own un-assuming way he single-handedly introduced a strong Pentecostal Charismatic influence into the United States Military. Long the preserve of the Episcopalian, Catholic and Lutheran chaplains' power-base, which held the monopoly of influence and power positions within the US Military chaplaincy, Colonel Jim Ammerman established the Chaplaincy of Full Gospel Chaplains (Pentecostal/Charismatic) in order to redress the ever-changing religious demographics among military personnel. Conservative estimates in religious demographics worldwide are as follows: Roman Catholics – 1.5 billion; Pentecostals – 588 million; Baptists – 105 million; Reformed – 105 million; Lutheran – 87 million; Anglican – 82 million; Methodists – 75 million; Presbyterians – 40 million; Non-Trinitarian – 27 million; Congregational, Free Churches, Anabaptists, Moravians etc. – 10 million. Jim Ammerman succeeded in helping the Department of Defense change the military by bringing it around to the reality the religious demographics.

"The opposition to Colonel Ammerman's advocacy for change was fierce and vehement, stemming from the long-standing denominational power-base in the chaplaincy. They didn't want their "over inflated" positions of importance eroded. However, with tenacious longevity, self-assurance and belief in his calling from God, Colonel Ammerman brought changes to the establishment. From the highest echelons of power in the Pentagon down to the lowest ranks in the military, ordinary enlisted men and women knew that their "Spirit Filled" faith in God would now be represented in the US Military by "Spirit-Filled" chaplains who would understand exactly what their spiritual needs required.

"I commend to you *Jim Ammerman In His Own Words* which will give you an insight into one of the greatest campaigners for the full gospel of Jesus Christ in recent times, about a man who held a position as one of the founding members of the board of trustees of Oral Roberts University, a man who has influenced not only the chaplaincy of the US Military, but also that of many other nations as well. I commend a man who loves God and has fulfilled the task that Christ Jesus has called him to fulfill, and that man is Colonel Revd. Dr. E. H. Jim Ammerman."

REV. STEPHEN J. HOUSTON, D.D., PH.D.
PRESIDING BISHOP, WORLD CONFERENCE OF METHODIST CHURCHES
LONDON, ENGLAND

"Inspiring and moving! This book will show you a different perspective of God's faithfulness, and power."

ROD SHEPHERD, D.D.
SENIOR PASTOR, THE CHURCH OF ABIDING LOVE
SPRING, TEXAS

The late Jim Ammerman has done an outstanding job in sharing his life story that even non-scholarly readers, who are largely unfamiliar with Military Chaplaincy, will have no trouble following. This book is a condensed version of how one man was used and made a difference in our military and the lives of thousands of the highest-ranking officers and soldiers in our nation. This story of the late Dr. Jim Ammerman is a remarkable account of his faith, his hope and his dedication to transform the military chaplaincy. It is the story of a man, his foundation, and his education, devoting his life for a cause higher than his. As you read his words you will see that he lived according to the Word of God. He was not just a religious man, but a godly man. His life mattered and his influence reached around the world. This book not only gives us insight to make our count, but challenges us to believe God can answer our prayers above all that we can imagine or think.

David A. Newberry D.D.

Preface

I first met Chaplain (COL) Jim Ammerman on Capitol Hill when we both petitioned Congress for chaplains' rights. Since that day Jim personally stood by me, and later defended my right to pray 'in Jesus' name' in uniform, even at great personal cost to himself and his own organization. When I was an outcast, he took me in, and defended me against the wolves. I'll never forget how much he loved Jesus, and freedom to speak His wonderful name. 'Not everybody prays in Jesus' name,' he said, 'but when the government says you can't, then you must.' Thank you Jim, for standing up for Jesus with me, no matter the cost.

Jim Ammerman was a great man of God. The goal of this book is to highlight his testimony and what the Holy Spirit has accomplished through this saint. What you are about to read, by and large, are the very words of Jim Ammerman in an interview he approved for publication. The transcription had to be edited for readability. Where incomplete sentences existed, complete sentences had to be formed with the use of brackets. Statements or portions of sentences or story lines that were not clear needed to be edited for clarity or deleted.

Any misrepresentation of Jim Ammerman's words or thoughts is purely unintentional. For I do not want to give the impression that Colonel Ammerman said specific words he did not utter. But overall the book is a quote of what Jim Ammerman said in a historic interview with Jim Linzey. I have edited out the questions during the interview, so as to capture the flow of thought of Jim Ammerman in his own words. Photos are included which highlight military ministry, which is what Jim Ammerman was all about. After all, one picture is worth one-thousand words.

Gordon J. Klingenschmitt, Ph.D.
May 2012

FOREWORD

I have had the honor of knowing Jim and Charlene Ammerman for many years. I've participated in some of the Chaplaincy of Full Gospel Churches conventions spearheaded by Jim and Charlene, I have been a sponsor of this outstanding chaplaincy commission for many years, we've worked together in the founding of Military Bible Association, Jim has endorsed my own books and he has endorsed my son, Dr. Jim Linzey, for the military chaplaincy. I was deeply honored when Jim and Charlene came to my honorary Doctor of Divinity ceremony when Jim was one of the keynote speakers in 2001. So I speak regarding Jim Ammerman and his influence with personal knowledge.

Perhaps the greatest impact of Jim Ammerman has been that of influencing the United States Armed Forces by establishing an umbrella military chaplaincy endorsing agency—Chaplaincy of Full Gospel Churches—targeting "full gospel" clergy in their respective denominations to make it possible for them to be military chaplains.

What Jim Ammerman stood for was "bigger than life," bigger than the United States Armed Forces, for his passion was serving Jesus Christ, and evangelizing the lost, and seeing the restoration and preservation of the American republic and culture, the propagation of truthful US history, and keeping Jesus Christ central to the American Dream.

An extremely intelligent and knowledgeable servant, Jim Ammerman thoroughly understood and articulated very well the dangers to the United States, causing so many people of every strata of society to seek him out and learn from him. Very few people know what Jim Ammerman knew or could articulate those truths, his philosophy, and the reality of what lies ahead for America unless Americans take courage and take a stand.

While Jim Ammerman's mission on earth was multifaceted, this book focuses on personal experiences, his calling to the ministry, and some of the things he was able to accomplish through the military chaplaincy, both in the United States and South America. We deeply miss Jim Ammerman, since his passing last year on my birthday, May 17, 2011.

From a little farming community in Conway, Missouri, here is the story of the supernatural life of an ordinary man, *Jim Ammerman: In His Own Words*.

Verna M. Linzey, D.D.
May 2012

DEDICATION

To

Charlene Ammerman

Table of Contents

Acknowledgements VII
About Jim Ammerman VIII
Preface XVII
Foreword XIX
Dedication XXI
Chapter 1:   Everybody Ought to Know: 3
Chapter 2:   Where We Go From Here: 15
Chapter 3:   Reflections of the Past 19
Chapter 4:   Expanding to South America 25
Chapter 5:   Personal Challenge. 33
Chapter 6:   My Calling 37
Chapter 7:   Military Ministry 43
Chapter 8:   Conclusion 53
Recommended Reading 55
Prayers of the United States Armed forces 57
Hymns of the United States Armed Forces. 67
The Armed Forces Believers' Creed 73
Creeds of the United States Armed Forces 75
Core values of the United States Armed Forces 81
U.S. Military Code of Conduct 85
U.S. Military Oaths of office 87
The Pledge of Allegiance 89
The Covenant and the Code of Ethics for
           Chaplains of the Armed Forces 91
The Role of Military Chaplains 95
The Meaning of Marriage 97
The ten commandments as The Foundation of America . . . 101
King Solomon Refutes communism 107
Leadership Quotes on Religious freedom 109
How General Ralph E. Haines, Jr.,
           Received the Baptism with the Holy Spirit . . . 117

U.S. COAST GUARD CHAPLAINS PRAY WITH PRESIDENT GEORGE W. BUSH

"Therefore I exhort first of all that you make supplications, prayers, intercessions, and thanksgivings for everyone, for kings and for all who are in authority, that we may lead a quiet and peaceful life in all godliness and honesty" (I Tim. 2:1-2, MEV). Fifty-two Navy chaplains serving in the U.S. Coast Guard lift the spirit of President George W. Bush during their historic visit with their commander-in-chief on the White House South Lawn on 9 May 2003. U.S. Navy photo (Released)

Chapter 1

Everybody Ought to Know
Beginnings of Chaplaincy of Full Gospel Churches

We started this Chaplaincy [of Full Gospel Churches (CFGC)] twenty-nine years ago, and it has grown. God knew how big it was going to be, but I would never have believed it if you told me back then. We have over five hundred and twenty chaplains now. That includes not only the U.S. military, where most of them are, but it includes the VA hospitals, and state and federal prisons, and other institutions. We even have chaplains in some universities. But what I have encouraged all our chaplains to do is not to grow stale on Jesus, but to stay abreast of things, build a good library, be true professionals in the best spiritual sense of that word, and always make the number one book the Bible. And Jim Linzey, of course, is a specialist in that area because he has produced another Bible that is going to be of great service to leaders. And we need to know that. And we need to enhance that [endeavor], any of us, any way we can.

Spiritual Leadership

But real leadership, always, in America, will include the spiritual dimension. Now we're about to lose our Constitution. I think most of you hearing this or reading this later in print will know that. We're not about to lose our Constitution. God raised up this nation, and God is not going to let this nation go down the drain. I do not care what some people's plans are for a one-world government and all that. In fact, we may be the hub and the center.

We have a tremendous lawyer—a constitutional lawyer. And I know other constitutionalists. We are not going to let our Constitution be wiped out for the one-world crowd, as much as they want it to be, though they have many people in primary places, including high places in Washington, DC. We all need to understand our heritage. We need to listen to people like Dave Barton, who really knows the original intent of the founders of this nation, or Bill Federer. Dave is right here in Fort Worth, Texas, just on the west side. Bill Federer is in St. Louis. And both of them are great constitutionalists, born again, and [men who are] fully filled with the Spirit. So God has not left us without leadership in that dimension.

But we have an attorney just at the edge of Washington, DC, and we walked the halls of Congress and got things changed when they said chaplains could not pray in the name of Jesus. And he, and the endorser for one of the Independent Baptist groups, who is a great man out of South Carolina, is in touch with the senator from South Carolina, who helped make sure that we didn't lose the Jesus connection in our chaplaincy in any of these institutions. And there are other people like Ron Ray of North Carolina [who] is a retired full colonel U.S. military lawyer. God has raised up people to safeguard this very unique document called the United States Constitution.

IMPRIMIS

He has even raised up an institution called Hillsdale College up in Michigan. There are 1,800,000 people who receive this [publication] each month. It is called the *Imprimis*, which means "the first things." I hold in my hand their latest publication. They have speakers who speak there and other places including cruise ships. This one is entitled "The Coming Constitutional Debate." The U.S. Government could not have anything to say about them or their students. Not only do they not accept any educational money from the government at any state or federal level, [but] they do not allow their students to accept any government money. [But Soldiers, Marines, Sailors, Airmen, and Guardians, who have earned the GI Bill may use that to attend without being forced to listen to the one-worlders. Apparently, some judges thought these students ought to have to listen to the one-world crowd for receiving government funds. But] they've raised extra money and kept their tuition low [and are helping] veterans pay their tuition at their own institution. So they can still go to school there and not lose their GI Bill.

Folks, we have many people across this land, more than [half of whom have risen] up and are really being heard. [But *Imprimis* is] being [read] by almost two million people every month. And as soon as it [is sent to me], I always [ignore] all the rest of the mail and read their publication because they put it in print. You can also receive it by disk if you want to or tape. But we need to know that our freedoms are about to be lost here in America. And over the noon meal just today, my wife and I were discussing at the table [that I'll be eighty-five] in July. I am not worried about my future too much because most of my future is going to be in heaven. [When] I married, I robbed the cradle. I was twenty years old and came back from World War II, four years into the War and married [Charlene.] She was eighteen. She is two years younger than [I am.] And we have now been married for sixty-five years. And it is our children and our grandchildren that we are thinking about.

Spiritual Future

And those of you hearing this or reading this need to know that you need to think about the future of your family. Because, let me tell you, while we may not be too involved in a one-world government, our children and grandchildren—our progeny—are going to be, unless we stand up now, as patriots. I am a patriot. I am a veteran of three wars: World War II in the Navy as first radioman and then as a pilot; and secondly, Korea; and thirdly, Vietnam. And I was there twice. I was there and went across the border the second time. We were allowed by the President to sweep into Cambodia; that was a sanctuary for the North Vietnamese Army. They could hit us and run back across there and we could not get them. So the president allowed us to do a fifteen-day sweep over into Cambodia and Laos. We went over and got those rascals who had a sanctuary where they were torturing our American military [men] whom they had captured. And [we] freed all of them. And I know it was a life-risking thing.

God Cares for His Own

But let me say this to you to encourage your heart. If God puts you somewhere, then you ought to know that He takes care of His own. Don't you ever forget that. I have lived through three wars, on the land, the sea, and in the air. I don't have a mark from the wars on my physical self. I don't even have a mark on my psychological self. I never had PTSD because I knew what God's call was. [Whom] God calls, He protects and nurtures. And so if God calls you to some unusual ministry, and it is a dangerous one, do not consider it dangerous, because He still keeps His eye upon His servants and upon this planet called Earth, and especially upon America—freedom loving people. And that's why this leadership Bible is so important. Those of us who are leaders are going to go through the fire. I have been through it. And I have a lawsuit against me right now that I am not free to talk about. Now "he" talks about it and publishes about it. A man does not like it because our chaplains are such soul winners. That is his problem. It is not mine. And the court case is his problem; it is not mine. But I do not intend to violate the court's decree or the judge's decree. This is to be kept out of the news. And he has not kept it out of the news. Some of you know what I am talking about. I did not name this man, and I don't name him. Wait until the trial is over.

Anyway, I know that what we have done has been legal, and it will be proven as such in the courts of the land. Then no one can challenge it. And Jim Linzey has been a part of standing up for the Lord at all costs. It does not matter what the price is. Nobody has nailed me to an old rugged cross yet, although I have had some pretty serious things happen. I was locked up incommunicado one time for five months while I was on active duty because of some unbelieving chaplains. I can talk about that because that is all past history, and I was proven totally [to be] in the right.

[On another occasion,] I had exercised my constitutional rights. I had Bob Jones come and preach. And I tried to get them to let me bring Billy Graham on one of the larger posts—Fort Campbell, KY. It was not commanders that kept me from bringing those two great evangelists on. It was unbelieving chaplains. Jim, I hope you heard me. It was unbelieving chaplains that kept me from that.

Green Beret Chaplain

But an interesting thing happened while I was a Green Beret chaplain over in Europe. This was part of my training for later to bring chaplains in, the right kind of people—men and women of all races and descriptions. The only Americans we have not been able to get in are American citizens from America Samoa.

I have had some of the chiefs as chaplains, of more restrictive denominations, say, "Where do you get all these people?" And one of them was a Missouri Synod Lutheran. And I said, "I'll tell you what. I will meet you on Sunday morning in your area." In this case, it was Bolling Air Force Base where the Air Force headquarters was. And he was Chief of Chaplains. "And I will give you a list of all our chaplains within a hundred miles. And I'll give you a list of all our churches within a hundred miles. You tell me which service you want to visit on that Sunday morning, and we will go in their congregations—in the military or civilian life. When you walk in there, you can see their people from all races and tribes and speeches, because that's who we minister to. That is who Christ died for. And we know that we're on the right track. We're following in the footsteps of Jesus and so are all our people."

And he declined to do that, because they have a very restrictive approach and he was not allowed to even attend services like that. And I said, "You would see where we get our people. They are from the churches that our people minister to. People come up and hear the call of God for them to be a chaplain. And they respond to it, and we support them. We open the door for them and support them as long as they're a chaplain, and after when they retire." So God is doing a great thing.

Educated and Intelligent Chaplains

Through that, one of them in one of the services, and I'll not identify him further, he wouldn't want me to, they found out in his first assignment that he was sharper than anybody else in the chaplaincy of that service (of the Army, Air Force, Navy or Marines). The Navy furnishes the Marines. But anyway, the Chief of Chaplains of that branch called me and said, "We're about to give him his first assignment after his initial assignment. And I do not know where to utilize all this man's talents."

I had to say to that two-star Chief of Chaplains, "You can't. This man is gifted far beyond anything that has happened in any service. So just assign him to one of the tougher places, with a greater challenge, and he will do a great job and give the chaplaincy the credit. He is that humble of a man"—a man that had a Ph.D. from Pat Robertson's [Regent University], who said he wanted to come on active duty. He named the service. And I said, "They'll accept you, although they may have a small acceptance this month. But they will accept you, because your record is so strong."

And they called me and said, "We've never had a man with a file this strong." And the man that called me was of that service, and he said, "I've been doing this for fifteen years, setting up these boards, and I've never seen a file like this. And we have sixteen times as many applicants for one space this month that we'll have, and your man will get that."

And I said, "How do you know?"

That is when he said, "I've done this for fifteen years, and I know how to read the boards before they meet. He is such a terrific person." And here he is ready to go overseas.

And the Chief of Chaplains of that service called me and said, "How do I utilize this man?"

And I said, "I don't think you can in any service."

Well he got assigned to NATO Headquarters. Now, remember, he had been a chaplain for only two years. And when he got there, he called me and said that [they had him preach once every three months]. And he said [to them], "Can I have the sanctuary one night a week to preach the gospel as I understand it?"

[The answer he received was], "Well, the only night we have free is Tuesday. And that is not a real good night to draw a crowd."

He had so many people going on Tuesday night. I don't mean [in a] Sunday school room, I mean the sanctuary in the main post chapel.

Special Assignment

And so, on the Wednesday after the second Tuesday night, the four-star general at that base had his chief of staff, a full colonel, send for this man. [The chaplain] called me and said, "Am I in trouble? The chief of staff of the four-star general has just called me to report to the four-star immediately."

And I called him by his first name, and I said, "You will never be in trouble. You are such a humble servant of God. Call me when the meeting is over. In the meanwhile, I'll be on my knees in the back office where nobody will bother me, praying for you as you go in to see him."

And he called me in about forty-five minutes, and he said that when he got there, the four-star said, "Give me a summary, a half hour summary, on what you've been teaching the last two Tuesday nights. My wife has been in that class."

Well, he did not know who the wives were. You know, he was the newbie. And he said, "Well, sir, did I offend her any?"

"Oh no," he said, "she is wild about what you're teaching. And I want a summary of it."

And the chaplain said, "I gave him a thirty-minute summary."

And he said, 'I am a four-star general over one-third of the service. I am calling all the generals in, a hundred of them, and I want you to speak to them and give them this teaching—a summary of it.'

And he said, "Now I am nervous."

And I answered, "Let me put it on my calendar, and I'll stop by the office, and we'll pray for that hour. And then call us when it is over."

And when it was over, he asked, "Do you understand the term 'corona committee?'"

And I answered, "Yes, I do. [That is a meeting of] all the four-star generals in that particular service—the flag officers."

"Oh, now," he said, "I am nervous. I'm to speak to them next week."

Scripture Brings Hope

And they had the Surgeon General of that service, who was a three-star, there. Remember there was a rash of suicides going on a couple of years ago. Well, it was during that time that the Surgeon General was there and he spoke to the four-star generals when our chaplain finished and said, "This hopeful teaching from the Scripture of God will stop the suicides in our land." And he was put on orders to produce the latest method of dispensing a message. And everybody in that service was required to hear it.

Some of them went to the judge advocates and said, "We are being marched to service, a religious service. And we're going to complain to the Inspector General." They complained to the Inspector General.

And the top flag officer in that service said, "When we have an emergency, and suicides are an emergency, a commander can do anything he needs to do to stop it. And that is what he is stopping. And don't let anybody get in the way of this man."

God's Plan for Everyone

And so they know that we have done what I said we would do thirty years ago when I went before the Armed Forces Chaplains' Board that approves endorsers. They said, "Where are we going to get any of your kind? Where can we get any of your kind that even meets basic requirements?" And these were all flag officers, two stars each. Now I have already retired, but I have stood in the presence of many generals. During the last half of my twenty-six-year service, I was on general officer staffs where there would be maybe three to five generals. And I would say, "Gentlemen, this book that I believe in says that none of you need to miss heaven. God has a plan for every one of you to have one of the mansions in heaven." And they had never been told that. And so I led many of those senior officers to the Lord. They had never had a chaplain tell them about Jesus.

I learned a little song that came out while I was still a young teenager—"Everybody Needs to Know." I had a pastor in Kansas City, Kansas, that taught his church that song. And I was going to that church at that time. I met a girl there, and she was fourteen when I met her. I married her four years later. That was sixty-five years ago. And I liked that song because it is true. "Everybody Needs to Know" who Jesus is.

U.S. AIR FORCE HONOR GUARD

"I thank my God, always mentioning you in my prayers, whenever I hear of your love and faith, which you have toward the Lord Jesus and for all the saints, that the sharing of your faith may be most effective by the acknowledgement of every good thing which is in you from Christ Jesus" (Phm. 1:4-6, MEV). The U.S. Air Force Honor Guard drill team joins in prayer before the performance January 21, 2011 at the Boys and Girls Club of D.C., Washington D.C. The prayer brings the team together to motive them before the performance. U.S. Air Force photo by Senior Airman Christopher Ruano (Released)

Chapter 2

Where We Go From Here
Education is Important for Growth

Jim, I am in a retirement center now—my wife and [I are]. We have a very nice apartment. We have three meals a day, and my wife does not need to cook or do the dishes or anything. Housekeepers even come in and clean our apartment. We have two bedrooms, so we can have a guest couple. In there, I have a roll-top desk and one end-opening file cabinet. I have downsized from five file cabinets, and from 10,000 books down to one bookshelf that goes all the way to the top of one room. I cried over that. Books have always been my friends. I hold several degrees, because I did what our chaplains have been encouraged by me to do. And I've said, "Don't go stale on Jesus. Get yourself a good library. Go to professional conferences. Be a somebody in the kingdom that no one can refute." And so our chaplains, again and again and again, have said, "Well, if I'm going to do that, I might as well get a doctorate." And Jim Linzey is one of those.

And I spoke to the Armed Forces [Chaplains'] Board—not the one that approved me originally. They had all retired and quit work and quit preaching in the main. Most of them just totally retired. And I said, "When are you going to start accepting off-campus degree work?" There were three of them there—two-star gentlemen—and they told me that they never, never would. One right after the other! And I said, "Then you're out of step with the American educational system, because Yale and Harvard and Princeton are all offering off-campus degrees at every level. Our people are going to come up with those degrees." And they have and they still are enrolled in degree work, and are taking it out of their sleep time and all maybe to get it done.

But now, off-campus degree work is fully accepted by the Armed Forces [Chaplains'] Board. They called me and said—and you'll be happy to know this, Jim—that we have more people on Active Duty with earned doctorates from accredited universities and seminaries than the next two denominations put together. Well, that's our people. And they're wondering [if] we have anybody qualified. Our people are leading the way. Yes, they are. And I am proud of them—every one of them. I am encouraging them. Some of them say, "I'm going to go ahead and get a doctorate before I apply for Active Duty."

God takes willing people, and brings them all the way to the top. And I have encouraged Jim Linzey every way I know how to encourage him, because I expect him to go to the top and be not just a nationwide leader. He has worldwide capability! I know he is listening to this recording.

Chaplain Jim Linzey Preaches at Leader's Training Course

"If you remain in Me, and My words remain in you, you will ask whatever you desire, and it shall be done for you" (Jn. 15:7, MEV). Chaplain, Major Jim Linzey preaches John 15 to ROTC cadets at the U.S. Army Cadet Command's Leader's Training Course 2006 at Fort Knox, Kentucky, as the institution's first full-time chaplain. Photo: Courtesy of LTC Public Affairs Office (Released)

Chapter 3

Reflections of the Past
God Uses Chaplains and Seminaries

One of the things we kept from that large house [on Whitewood Drive in Dallas], when we downsized into this retirement community, was an oil painting made from a little colored snapshot.

When the Depression started, my father had a good job. He was running a big grocery store in Detroit. But suddenly, people could not buy groceries. We saw them eating out of our garbage cans. That was the start of the Great Depression. And he said, "We're going back where I grew up, to a farm where we can raise our own food, because people, when they get so anxious, will kill you for the groceries in your pantry." And he said, "I do not want to be in Detroit," which was one of the cities first hit by the Great Depression. Men were standing in line to [buy] an apple, to take one apple home for their family—stuff like that. I saw that as a five-year-old boy.

I went to kindergarten in Detroit, Michigan. And by the way, it was an integrated school. And I learned to believe in integration—racial integration—in our schools, while I was in kindergarten.

Isn't that interesting? God has His way of having you ready ahead of time for what's coming down the road. And we have a fully integrated [gender-integrated chaplaincy].

INTEGRATION OF CHAPLAINCY

We have women chaplains. [But the military] does not know what to do with all of them. Some of them have even served over in the desert in combat units. And they've done well. The services have learned how to take care of them. And the services just announced this past week that they are going to put women on submarines. Boy, that is close integration, where your bunk is under a bunk! If a person is a little overweight, you cannot turn over without touching [the bunk above you.]

I served on a destroyer for thirteen months where that was true. It was all male at that time, and we had only a few places we could take a shower. I do not know how the services have adjusted to all this. But I have seen it in the Army as an Army chaplain. They made adjustments where women could have a tub to take a bath in instead of just all showers, and where they have a kitchen to cook in if they wanted to. I said to my three-star boss that I was serving directly with at that time, "We have some men that like to cook. You're going to have to put kitchens where they can cook, too."

He said, "You think so?"

I said, "I guarantee it."

A committee of men showed up the next day and said, "We want there to be kitchens for us to cook in also."

And [the General] called me and said, "I think you ought to be here for this time."

And I said, "We're going to have to do it. If we do it for the ladies, we have to do it for the men. This reverse discrimination cannot work." So that is where Jim Ammerman has been on the cutting edge of all this. God has placed me there.

EFFECTIVENESS OF CHAPLAINS

This [General] was a Presbyterian who started the day by reading his Bible. And I have been with him in his office reporting in for fifteen minutes when he said, "Let us sit over here, side-to-side, on this divan. He had the office [General Dwight D.] Eisenhower had when he came over from England. And, man, it was a big place and it was well equipped.

[General] Eisenhower had said, "Don't bomb that building. It is owned by the biggest chemical company that Hitler has." [Hitler] was producing all the stuff to kill the Jews at that time. "Don't bomb that building. Save that building for my headquarters."

Now my commander had that. And he said, "Let us sit on this divan over here. His office was larger than our living room and kitchen put together, now. And I was sitting there, and he said, "Now, listen to this." What an indictment on chaplains! This was the first week of July. And he said, "Thirty-three years ago last month, I graduated from West Point. Thirty-three years ago! And I've looked for a chaplain for thirty-three years that could be my pastor. And he walked in this morning." And I wept, because he had not found a chaplain worthy of being his chaplain, because he loved the Lord and probably knew the Bible better than most of [the chaplains] knew it. And he said, "I think he walked in this morning."

VERSATILITY OF CHAPLAINS

And I knew we could change all evils. He had outfits where Soldiers were sleeping in German parks in their sleeping bags, because it was not safe, because of junkies and so forth. The race riots were taking place. And there were concerns about [the accommodations] that his troops were occupying— built by the Germans, right after the war. And I had visited those at night and some of the commanders were afraid to go see their men at night. It was not safe. They would kill the commanders, and they tried to kill one. They had knifed him and thrown him out a window onto a cobblestone street twenty feet below. They threw him through the window!

They were up for trial when I got to that command, and I said, "That will change in six months! And there will be spiritual change, or I'll retire to get out of this kind of an environment, because I refuse to be a part of a command where that can happen to troops."

And he said, "We'll both do it together."

And I knew then we were not going to have to retire or resign. With the commander saying, "We'll do it together," I knew we could change those hundred thousand people in six months.

And I prayed about it, and God sent me a hundred thousand Bibles. I said, "Most people with a high school [education] cannot read or understand the King James Version. I want a Living Bible, Old and New Testament."

And, would you believe, God had a hundred thousand delivered to me out of Tyndale House. They said, "Trucks will roll up from the port to your place in Frankfurt, and there'll be a hundred thousand Bibles on them for you to pass out."

That is the power of prayer, folks. God sent them to me. No charge, even for delivering them! What had happened was that the chaplain who had been under me during the big push of the war over in Vietnam was now the chief of staff for Dr. Ken Taylor who owned Tyndale House Publishers. And he said, "Who are these to go to, Dr. Ken?"

And he said, "Oh, some guy named Jim Ammerman."

And the chaplain said, "Oh!" And [he told Dr. Ken that "Jim Ammerman] had to ship them from the USA to Germany."

And [Dr. Ken] said, "No, he does not. We will pay for that."

He was my senior chaplain the first time I was in combat. And when we were told to take a hill, we took thirteen hundred casualties. They were not killed, though many were hospitalized. This chaplain came up and stayed with me. And we prayed over every one of those before they went up that hill. And we had so few casualties compared to what the Pentagon expected. They could not believe it, because God protected those soldiers.

And I had a young chaplain who stayed in only three years. He came back to Fort Polk, Louisiana, which is not a post that many people ask for. But that is where they assigned him. While he was there, he called me and said, "Ken Taylor wants me to come, and I'm educated enough to be his editor-in-chief. They're publishing these in the garage and shipping them out wrapped in used paper. And I have three little girls to raise. What do you think I ought to do?"

And I said, "You hear from God, and if God says go do it, you go do it. And He'll feed your children and send them through college." So he did.

Folks, God is greater than we know. Most of us never understand who Jesus really is. He sits there at the right hand of the Father. Folks, I do not know if you have ever stood up again when kicked down. But Jesus is seated at the right hand of the Father, making intercession for you and me. And so I do not worry who it is who I am to see during the next visit.

CHAPLAIN GLENN BROWN BAPTIZES US MARINES

"Can anyone forbid water for baptizing these, who have received the Holy Spirit as we have?" (Acts 10:47, MEV). Commander Glen Brown, Chaplain Corp, USN, one of the US Navy's most influential chaplains, baptizes Marines in Okinawa in 1974. Commander Brown was the senior chaplain and Regimental chaplain at Camp Hansen. Colonel Alfred Gray, who was the Camp Commanding Officer and Regimental Commander, later became a Four-Star General and Commandant of the US Marine Corps. (U.S. Navy Photo)

Chapter 4

Expanding to South America
Seminaries Continue to Multiply

Almost every congressman and senator three years ago, in their offices, made a decision that chaplains could pray in Jesus' name, and that they could not be stopped from it. I took an attorney with me to see one senator. That is the way you get in to see these people since they are all lawyers. They speak legalese. And so if you have a good, born again, Spirit-filled lawyer, take him with you to see these congressmen and senators. And you will get what you want. First of all, you get in to see them. I had my lawyer take notes. I said, "Art,"—and Jim, you know Art—"I do not care what you write. It may be a list for shopping. You might need food for the dog or your lawn mowed. But do not let them see it. Just write notes, and they will think you are taking notes on what we are talking to them about. Then they will keep their promises." And they did. Praise God! So if I ever have to go to Washington, D.C., again, I will have him with me. He will be taking notes, and they will do what we ask.

God Works through Men

God did not make us smart people [just in order for us] to act ignorantly. God gave me an IQ. I did not know what an IQ was until I was in the flight program for the Navy. They gave us an IQ test. We kid the Texas Aggies about being dumb, calling it a QI test—Questionable Intelligence! That is just the way we treat Texas Aggies down here. I have two or three in the family that have doctorates. They are medical and veterinarian doctors from Texas A&M. But I kid them about Questionable Intelligence.

The fact is, we have a man who is president of our seminary in South America [Seminary for Chaplaincy of Full Gospel Churches]. I am going to keep him there in that position. I took him to South America with me. I initially thought he was a Mexican. I do not speak enough Spanish to go down there without an interpreter. So I took him along. And I met the military leaders of ten nations from South America, and five nations from Central America. They wanted to talk with me about a born again, Spirit-filled, non-Catholic chaplaincy. God arranged that. But I needed a good translator. I took him along. He was born in Caracas, Venezuela. I did not know that. He is married to a Mexican-American legal citizen. He could be a full citizen. But it takes us a little longer to come and go because he is a green-card citizen. He has kept his citizenship in Caracas, Venezuela. And because of that, that president down there [President Hugo Chavez], who cannot remember my German name—Ammerman—calls me "the white-haired guy from Dallas, Texas."

But he had a meeting with the three hundred people he rules that nation with and said, "This man has been coming down here and educating our people. He has done only good and has not asked us for a single thing."

Our seminary down there, graduate level, is approved and accredited through doctors on the international scene, because I said, "If we start a seminary here, we'll go first class. I do not have a second class Jesus." And folks, you need to hear that. You do not have a second class Jesus. So everything you do in His name should be done first class.

Seminary Provided For

In six years, we were fully accredited. This man had his Ph.D. degree from Texas A&M, and that helped. He is a citizen in Venezuela. So he could not hold a full citizenship here. We do not allow that. And so he is a green-card citizen here. He comes and goes, and it takes time to get in and out of the country. But we spend that time, when we come and go, because I want him to be accepted in Venezuela, primarily due to his position as president of our seminary there. The president said that we have been given money. They have one oil well there. America buys seventeen per cent of the oil that we need from them. They have that much oil.

[Our ministry in Venezuela] has been given three pieces of land. And the best is ten acres inside the city limits of Caracas, just a block off of their subway in that mountainous town. You can ride their subway system clear across the city for six or eight cents. And some people commute to seminary and live at home. But anyway, there are those ten acres, and we already had paid for a complete set of blueprints to include the shrubs and trees. It will be the nicest piece of property in the city, so that even the two Catholic Archbishops in that city could say, "We may not like his theology, but he sure builds a nice home base seminary." And they are going to say that about us because it will be the nicest educational [institution] in the city. But Venezuelans have one big well pumping on the corner of their university in Caracas. Citizens of that land can go all the way through university without paying a cent for their education, because of the oil from that one deep well.

The Lord Provides

The Lord woke me up—and nobody knows this except my own family—woke me up two weeks ago in the middle of the night and said one thing: "You already have the money for building that seminary." The estimated cost down there is ten million dollars. It would be a lot more here. Things are cheaper there.

I have a retired four-star general. His wife is retired from being the executive secretary to three presidents. She can run the country. They are born-again, Spirit-filled. They both graduated from our seminary. And I said, "Why are you going to seminary? You're in your middle fifties. You're heroes in the land. And everybody knows you. Why?"

And they said, "God has told us that as long as we live, we're to work for that seminary to see that it is run right, at no expense to you, because we do not need the money."

That is the way God provides for His own. So they will see that we do not get cheated or anything else. They can get in to see the president any time they want to. We are going to approach him about possibly having the oil revenue from one of those pieces of land. God said, "That's the money that will build your home base seminary, mother seminary land.

I was wondering where the ten million dollars would come from to send down there. But we do not have to worry about that. I hadn't thought about that. But that land has oil under it. Oil is not the main income of that nation. The main income of that nation is aluminum. Many of those mountains have the kind of soil that one could make aluminum out of. I haven't touched on it, but there is someone helping subsidize the expense of our overseas seminary.

Branches in Mexico

Mexico wanted three branches of the seminary, because it is such a big nation with such a big population. I just made a trip down to Monterrey. I had been in Monterrey in 1951, and it was just a mountain town with almost nothing. It was just a village. Now, it is a city of four million people, a very prosperous, rich city, with a downtown shopping area that looks like downtown Chicago or downtown Dallas. And I asked, "How did all this happen?"

They said, "You see all these rocky mountains down here?"

I said, "Yes."

And they said, "They're the kind of rocks that, when you grind them up, make the best cement in the world. And we can sell it all to China, because they cannot get enough to build."

And now this is a rich city of four million people. Out of that wealth came a seminary. But now the Catholics do not have anyone to go to seminary. And so we learned in Caracas that if they do not have anyone to go to their seminaries, they will lease them to us [less expensively] than it would cost us to own them—if they gave them to us. They cannot give them to us, because it is in the deed that they revert back to the company or rich family that gave the money to build the seminaries. So they have to keep them. We have learned this, going to other countries, including Nicaragua, and some others down there, where we already have seminaries. We go in there and ask, "Where are your seminaries that are vacant and not being used?" And they tell us, gladly. We say, "Take us over there." So we have the use of a tremendous place in Caracas, including nice dorm rooms—every one with a bathroom and so forth. And we are renting them for less than what it would cost if they gave them to us. And they have them staffed, including the kitchens. And they have good food. And so we are being underwritten by the Catholic Church. So listen—take those things that are given by someone, in some position, to be used for God. And we'll use it for God better than anyone they ever heard of. And so we are not violating what those people want and cherish. We are giving beyond what they thought they wanted.

SEMINARIES SPREAD THROUGH SOUTH AND CENTRAL AMERICA

We have a request to put an evangelical chaplaincy in the ten nations of South America and the five nations of Central America.

And [those chaplains] are to be graduates of our seminaries that we have set up down there. And we do it all, and it is subsidized by the Catholic Church. Talk about God knowing how to do business! Watch for God who wants to bless you in some ways you have never expected. And then He woke me up in the night and said, "You already have the resources for that ten million dollar home base seminary."

And I said, "Well, God, I sure don't know it."

And He said, "That is why I woke you up. And the only reason I woke you up is—there is oil under the land that is already in your name. And so you already possess it."

Now I think I will have to go see the president and give him a written statement guaranteeing that I will never take a penny of that oil money outside of his country. But I do not want it for outside of his country. I want it for that home base seminary—for the Spanish speaking world. And so God is getting ready to continue doing these things.

U.S. AIR FORCE CHAPLAIN LEADS PILOTS IN PRAYER

"Therefore, brethren, diligently make your calling and election sure. For if you do these things, you will never stumble" (II Pet. 1:10, MEV). Operation Enduring Freedom -- A U.S. Air Force chaplain leads pilots and crewmembers from Charleston C-17 Globemaster III at Charleston Air Force Base, S.C., in prayer prior to takeoff. Airmen from Charleston continue high altitude drops of Humanitarian Daily Rations from their C-17 Globemaster IIIs somewhere over northern Afghanistan. The C-17 dropped 17,220 HDRs. About a half million HDRs have been dropped into Afghanistan since the humanitarian relief effort began. U.S. Air Force photo by Mannie Garcia, Gannett, ATPCo (Released)

Chapter 5

Personal Challenge
My Health

I had everything lined up for a kidney transplant. I am on dialysis every Monday, Wednesday, and Friday. It takes fifteen hours out of my work week by the time I leave here, go to the clinic, get the treatment and get back home. And I do not need fifteen hours a week for taking care of kidneys that I inherited. I did not kill my kidneys with riotous living.

Jim, you're hearing a man talk now that has never smoked a cigarette, that has never taken an alcoholic drink, because I grew up in a Baptist deacon's home, and he taught me right on these things. And so I should not have kidney problems, but it is in our family tree. It killed my father at sixty-eight. I will be [eighty-five] this July. But I am on dialysis. I have the best kidney doctor. He is the most experienced. He has done twenty-five hundred kidney transplants, and he is going to be my surgeon. I am glad God put me in touch with someone like that. This doctor said, "Normally, I would not do one on somebody your age; but I know what you're doing, and you're doing such great work for God." He is a Christian man right here in Dallas.

Would you believe, a young housewife whose husband I helped, who lost his foot, is coming to donate a kidney. He was with the Air Force as a refueling expert over in the desert. One foot was blown off of him with a mortar that came in. No one was taking care of him. And I got in touch with the director of the VA—an official who used to be the top general for the U.S. Army. So I had access to him at his headquarters in Washington, D.C., where now he is over the VA. [Later, we found out why this airman was not receiving the help he needed. His buddy was killed with that mortar that came in. The mortar had hit his buddy. Officials had confused this airman with his buddy. It was thought that the airman was killed. It was believed that he was dead. So officials wrote him a letter stating that the reason our VA has turned you down is because we have you listed as dead. Well it was his buddy that was killed rather than him.] And so we got that straightened out. But meanwhile, they thought he was some imposter who wasn't a veteran, trying to get free medical service from the VA. So they kept turning him down. We had him in three different places, and they would not take him. So we got all that cleared up.

So his wife said, "You were good to my husband." But that is not all. They live in Kansas City, Missouri, and she is coming down here to give a kidney for me. She has the same blood type and all-- "A" positive. I mean, God worked that out. They have two children. She is in the Army National Guard of the State of Missouri. [She wanted a job and wanted to be in the National Guard. Her husband was on Active Duty in the Air Force when she went into the National Guard. But she needed to be a part of the Guard that did not deploy.] Though the Missouri Guard is slated to leave soon to go to the desert, she is with [the Rear Detachment]—the headquarters when the main body deploys. She is a sergeant, and she has already cleared the operation with her commander, who told her to go ahead and give that man the kidney. And he told her to take time off as she needed it. So she will be coming down here.

My Tri-Care for Life has already approved $180,000.00 to take care of the operation. And it will not take that much. But I was complaining because that seemed awfully high-priced to me. I was talking to three doctors up in Medical City here in Dallas, and one of them had just come here from California. He is a Jewish man and a heart specialist. He said, "Do you know what the whole package costs for the donor and the recipient in California?"

I said, "I'm afraid to ask."

He said, "Three hundred thousand dollars in California."

I do not think the president understands medical expenses at all. Most people do not. But $180,000.00 is still the approved on the list. It does not have to be re-approved. The government will pay for her and for me. I will only have to pay for bringing her to Dallas.

Well, I just hope that you caught a vision greater than you previously had of who Jesus really is. If you work for Him with no questions asked, beyond the sky is the limit. The only limits are in heaven, and they are under his direct control. So you know there are no limits up there. I want each and every one of you that hear or read what I just said, to know that we have a great and mighty God, the only one of the universe. It still belongs to Him. And He is still going to run it.

SOLDIERS PRAY BEFORE CONVOY MISSION

"We know that if our earthly house, this tent, were to be destroyed, we have an eternal building of God in the heavens, a house not made with hands" (II Cor. 5:1, MEV). Troops kneel and pray in Iraq before going on a convoy mission. A convoy is an easy target for the enemy, who may wound or kill many Americans and destroy critical supplies. Photo: Courtesy of U.S. Army Public Affairs (Released)

Chapter 6

My Calling
God Speaks to Young People

When I was thirteen years old, our crops all burned up during the Depression in the dust bowl days. You read about that in history books now. But I lived through it as a boy. At nine years of age, the oldest of five boys and one girl, I did a man's work. Today, my father would be put in prison for allowing me to work like that. He bought another team of old mares, and I did a man's work. I was an average sized nine-year-old boy. He just let down the handles of all that walking farm equipment where I could reach them. But he very wisely had bought a team of old mares that had plowed all their life. They were smarter than I was. But today, officials would put my father in jail for mistreating a nine-year-old. But I was very proud of working. I was the only boy in my class that had his own team of mares. That was really something in a farming rural community.

God Speaks In Spite of Disaster

Our crops burned up the year I was nine in 1938. But be assured of this. The Lord spoke to me. I read the Bible through in ninety days. With the crops burnt up, I could not work in the fields. And so I read from daylight until it became dark. There was no electricity. We had kerosene lamps. Rural electrification came to America after World War II. We had electricity then. But I read from daylight until it became dark. In ninety days I read the Old and New Testaments. And I found out something that I had never heard preached on. And I knew the pastors personally at our church, because my father was one of the deacons. So the pastors were in our home regularly, off and on. And they used to take me with them to some of their pastors' conferences.

Like my grandfather, they knew God had placed a call on my life for ministry before I knew it. My grandfather on my mother's side was a great man of God. My middle name, Harmon, was after him. My mother was one of six red-headed girls, the youngest of six, and the baby of the family. She had two black-haired brothers, who were older. And I used to go to my grandfather's home, and my grandfather would have me read Scriptures to him. He was a real saint of God. And by the way, both my grandfathers were little boys during the American Civil War. The people of that generation were old men if they were forty-eight or fifty years old. Each one of my grandfathers lived to be ninety-two years of age. So I expect to live to be a hundred in this day with the art of medicine today. And I'll do it with the loan of a kidney on one side. I just tell you all these things, giving God the glory.

Education Accelerated

But I went to bed one night after we had prayer in that Baptist deacon's home. And I watched as my younger brothers came along. When they could put a sentence together, they prayed in the family circle. And they prayed from then on every night. Of course, I learned to read at five years old. So I finished high school when I was fifteen, because I read everything in school. And while I was in grade school, they used to have us recite what our reading assignment was the last night. I could give the lesson for most of those grades, clear through eighth grade. And so I finished the eighth grade two years ahead of time and went on to high school. So I finished high school at fifteen and joined the Navy the day I was seventeen.

God Calls

When I was thirteen, after dad's prayer meeting downstairs, I went upstairs where I slept alone. There were a couple of other beds for the younger brothers. And I had the rest of the night—the Lord kept me awake. And He said, "If I am your Lord, then you have got to take orders from me. I am calling you into the ministry. You will teach Army officers about me."

I had planned to go in the Navy, and did go in the Navy. But, as a chaplain, I was an Army Chaplain. My endorser tried to get me to go into the Air Force or the Navy, because he had been my pastor when I was in preflight school in the Navy and he said, "You relate to these flyboys."

And I said, "No, George."

God Answers Prayer

In fact, Jim, I never did fill out an application for endorsement. Out of that telephone call he said, "We'll endorse you. I know you used to come to my home for Bible study when I was your pastor." That was when they had taken over Chapel Hill at Slate University. And he had a Bible study for those that wanted to learn more. And he said, "I know you, and you do not need to fill out any application. I'll just endorse you, but not for the Army."

Well, I could not tell him that God had awakened me and in a dream had made me take a parachute. And I had worn a parachute many hours but had never jumped in one. I had never seen one open. But I made one with a bunch of Soldiers from a very different plane that had twin booms instead of a fuselage. Later, when I went to the airborne school, guess what kind of a plane I jumped out of? One of those planes I had never seen. It was a C-119. We called them "a dollar 19." They would shake, rattle and roll like a bunch of tin cans. But that was the kind of plane that I jumped out of in my dream, though I had never seen a plane like that. Yet God gave me a full preview of it, and that was the kind I jumped out of in my first five jumps, and several later.

SAILORS PRAY

"Let every person be subject to the governing authorities, for there is no authority except from God, and those that exist are appointed by God" (Rom. 13:1, MEV). Sailors in Prayer, Naval Air Station North Island, San Diego, California, August 28, 2005—Sailors bow their heads as Captain Stanford E. Linzey, Jr., Chaplain Corp, USN (Ret.), leads in prayer before President George W. Bush speak at the 60th Anniversary of the Japanese Surrender in World War II. Photo by Chaplain Jim Linzey

Chapter 7

Military Ministry
We Learn and Grow

I passed all the tests while I was a radioman on a destroyer. When I was eighteen, the Navy immediately sent me back from the invasion of Sicily, which happened on my birthday. I was in an invasion that day. And they sent me back to become a naval aviator and pilot for the Navy. And it was then that I took an IQ test. I had never heard of an IQ test. They weren't common in those days. And they said, "Well, we only had a chart that went to a hundred and sixty-five, and you went off the chart. So we'll expect a lot out of you."

Twenty months later, the war had ended. Harry Truman, from my native state of Missouri, had dropped the big bomb, and that ended the war, because the Japanese were not ready to deal with that. They were ready to deal with killing a million Americans and giving up a million of their own men and women and children's lives to stop the invasion.

Reassigned to Teach the Japanese People

I came out of the Korean War, and I asked to be assigned to the occupation of Japan. The Japanese wanted to learn English so they could deal with the Americans. All our officers were educated people who still remembered Pearl Harbor and would not help them. But since I had two nights reserved to be my family nights, I said, "I'll take those two family nights and give you two hours a night and teach you English if you want to be a part of the land constabulary force." We were not going to give them even a motor boat and certainly not an airplane at that time. [A constabulary force is an armed police force that has been organized according to a military model, but it is separate from the army. It could be likened to a State Guard.]

[Similarly, American State Guards are under the governor, rather than under the president. For example, California and Texas both have the Air Guard and State Guard and the state's National Guard under the governor's control.] Texas has both Army and Air Guard. Like all states, these are placed under control of the president only if he needs to federalize them for national disasters or for war. Otherwise, he does not have these forces at his disposal. They train on military installations frequently. A lot of people in their respective states do not even know about this unless they are part of the Guard.

Teaching the Bible

[So, I taught them English if they would agree to be part of their constabulary force, which is loosely the equivalent of the Guard. And they had a huge tax on coffee.] Now they liked coffee, but they could not afford to buy it on their economy. So I taught them in the basement classroom of the chapel, and I had a big coffeepot, full, for them every night. Mainly, it was there to keep me awake, because I was putting in one-hundred hour weeks over there. But they also enjoyed the coffee. I had said, "If I teach you, it is going to include the Bible." And so I had bilingual Bibles that I received from the American Bible Society. And I taught them

Military Ministry

the Bible, and led many of them to the Lord. They were the future leaders of the military that Japan has today, and they were going to be Christians. There are ways to get things done for Jesus, if you look around and are willing to pay a little price for it.

But they were the ones that told me [that Japan had planned to lose ten million people in order to kill one million Americans]. I checked with our intelligence to see if they thought this was true. I found that our intelligence already knew it. In fact, I had a secretary, and she was in a girls' bamboo brigade. They were going to fight off American invaders on the beach with sharpened bamboo poles when she was in junior high school. Girls, old men with butcher knives, and stuff like that. They did not have guns, and there were no young men left on the mainland. They were all overseas, somewhere, fighting us, mainly out in the Pacific. And so I know that this is a true story—that they were willing to give up ten million of their people to kill one million American military men. But we did not have to face that, because of the "A" bomb. So I say, "Hooray for Harry Truman, who dropped the "A" bomb." I know it put us in the atomic age. But it saved eleven million lives. And so I say that was a pretty good trade off.

Chaplains Serving

By the way, under me were chaplains. Two of my chaplains were down in Hiroshima. The command I was in had the responsibility of providing food and supplying everything needed at Hiroshima, including the scientists and doctors that were there. One of the chaplains I had there later went to Germany on a ship. His wife went with him. That was back in the fifties. And I would go down to Hiroshima once a month to make sure everything was going all right with him. And it was not easy to minister to proud scientists in the front row in view of what has happened in the world, atomically. Also, it was not easy to minister to the doctors that were there to see what had happened to the victims from that blast. I had first-hand knowledge of Hiroshima and had a chaplain down there to minister to them, with his wife and daughter.

God Places Us to Serve

But, see, God uniquely placed me in all these things. I was in a lieutenant colonel's job, Jim, and I was still a lieutenant waiting to be a captain. The lieutenant colonel was a priest, and they caught him in bed with two [naked women]. His Catholic provost marshal [caught him], and the commander fired him and sent him back to the states.

[The number two chaplain] was a major, and a Southern Baptist, who could not stand the lax moral standards of the Orient. And they are very lax. They do not have any moral scruples about sex at all. And he thought he had a good assistant, and his wife thought she had a good live-in maid. We changed commanders. The old commander liked dinner dances, and he would stay until after midnight on Saturday night. Nobody dared leave until he left the Officers' Club, which had been built by the Japanese years before. He would have a good band or orchestra in there. So that meant that I had a short night's sleep the night before Sunday, when I had three services. But anyway, I dared not leave early.

Well the new commander said, "When we go out the front door, you and your wife are free to go home. We may come in the side door and eat and dance some more, but you do not have to stay up that late at night." And so he did that.

Serving Above Rank

The Southern Baptist chaplain and his wife went home early as I did this one particular night. I got a call shortly after I got home. I lived in the Kyoto Botanical Gardens. We had a beautiful home there, which was mowed and well kept. The trees had all the pine needles plucked out of every cluster by the Japanese until they had the minimum amount that made them look good. They were going to make it a botanical garden again since it was destroyed by the invasion. And my phone rang. It was the wife of the Southern Baptist chaplain. She said, "We got home and my husband flipped out. He does not even know his name. He left and I am worried about him." It was three o'clock in the morning, on Sunday morning. And she said, "I'm worried, and I've got little children here. I can't leave. Would you go find him?"

So I got in my uniform. We had three chapels over near where she was. So I began there. And sure enough, the one that he normally preached in had the lights on in it at three in the morning. So I went in there. This was the only time in my life I have ever seen a man pull the hair out of his head and throw it down. And he was walking up and down the aisle, mumbling incoherently, pulling the hair out of his head and throwing it on the carpet. I talked to him. He did not know his name; he did not know anything. But I took him home and I said to his wife, "I hope you have some strong sleeping pills."

She said, "Oh, I have trouble sleeping. I have some."

I said, "Give him a triple dose, and I'll put him in bed."

So we put him to bed, but I knew he was not going to wake up until after noon. And so I held his services the next morning. And on Monday, I went to the adjutant. Back then adjutants in the Army rated chaplains. Chaplains did not rate chaplains until I was a full colonel in the Army. They did in the other services.

And so I went to the adjutant to tell him what had happened. And he said "the commander is going to want to hear this from you."

So I went in, and when I finished, he said, "Okay, I'm cutting orders, and you're going to fill the lieutenant colonel's job and be my command chaplain."

I said, "Sir, that is not Army." We had thirteen chaplains and all of them were captains or above. But anyway, I had orders cut, and I was in a lieutenant colonel's job there.

Well the same thing had happened—not a moral issue involved—over in Korea. I arrived there, and a lieutenant colonel had had a stroke or a heart attack, and they flew him back to the general hospital of the Army in Tokyo. And I was the next one off the plane, and I was on the list for captain and didn't get promoted for two and a half more years. And that put me in a lieutenant colonel's job there, and I was in it fourteen months later when my tour was over.

Impact of Christians on the Military

Now again I'm in a lieutenant colonel's job in Japan, and I was there for two years, and then they sent me back to the States. And I said, "Sir, this isn't Army."

He said, "It's deeper cut into the Army than you think, Lieutenant."

I said, "Explain it to me, Colonel."

And he said, "I'm charged with carrying out my mission, with the assets I've been given. You're the only one who will get it done, although you have thirteen captains and two majors under you. And I know all of them, because I'm a Christian. And so I got acquainted with the chaplains as soon as I got here. And so you're the one who will get the job done, and, therefore, I'm doing what the Army says that I'm to do, and that is to take the assets they've given me and accomplish the mission."

Well, a full Colonel that didn't like me, a Catholic priest up in Tokyo, flew down from Tokyo with a four-star general to explain to my commander that he could not do that.

When it got approved for my family to join me in Japan, regulations said I could fly home and bring my family over. My wife had had breast surgery and came over with one arm in a sling and four kids to chase up and down the aisles for thirty-three hours with prop airlift. And he wouldn't let me go back to help them. Well I had a tough little wife, and she brought them anyway. And I was there to meet them when they landed in Tokyo, which he had not cleared. But I knew everybody and the monsoon was on. It was raining five inches an hour. And I went over the airfield, and I said, "If anything flies tonight, I need to get to Tokyo."

And they said, "We're having to fly a man out for a general court martial witness." But there was a foot of water on the airstrip. We were not sure we could take off. It was only prop planes then, and they didn't have the thrust of jets. And they said, "We'll put you on it, but it may not take off. It may get to the end of the runway and still be on the ground."

And so they [went, however slowly]. Finally, near the end of the runway, the water was only two or three inches deep, and they lifted off and pulled those wheels up out of that water. And I was over there to meet her plane when she got there.

God Answered Prayer

But you know, I had said to the folks, "We're going to go to Tokyo tonight."

"How do you know?" they asked.

And I said, "Because I have to be there tomorrow, and God knows that, and He is going to get us there."

And the pilot said, "Well, we're not that sure."

And I said, "If it helps you any, I was a pilot in World War II. It is not because I was a pilot that I say that. It is because I work for my boss in heaven first, and then I work for my boss on earth."

And they said, "Chaplain, let's get on the plane."

God Has Always Provided

Our lives have been this way—my wife and I. And I am saying to anyone that will hear this, "Sell out to the Lord." An exhaustive concordance will tell you, Jim, that the Bible says that Jesus is Savior thirty-two times, but it says he is Lord six hundred times.

Sell out to the Lord and make him the boss. Make him the Lord of your life, and do what He wants. Do not worry about the cost. He is rich in houses and lands. He holds the wealth of the world in His hands. He holds the oil, and He spends the oil in His hand. He holds the soil that will make aluminum. There is a thirteen-acre plot of land over there in the hills of Venezuela, another one with ten acres where we want to build there in the city limits, and another five acres of prime land. I already have in our Christian church name down there, three pieces of land that have the money on them, the wealth on them, to go ahead and build that home seminary base. That is the God that I serve and who wants you to serve Him. For all of you that hear this or read this, sell out to Him as the Lord of every bit of your life. And you will think heaven got loose on earth on your behalf.

GENERAL RALPH E. HAINES, JR., USA (RET.)
COMMANDING GENERAL, CONTINENTAL ARMY COMMAND

"I am confident of this very thing, that He who began a good work in you will perfect it until the day of Jesus Christ" (Phil. 1:6, MEV). General Ralph E. Haines, Jr., USA, now retired, reads Scripture in a military chapel. General Haines was the last Commanding General of the Continental Army. The first to hold this position was General George Washington, first president of the United States. Photo: Courtesy of U.S. Army Public Affairs (Released)

Chapter 8

Conclusion

From the heartland of America, Jim Ammerman was a traditional American with American Core Values. He represented the pulse of mainstream America in his beliefs, his life-long message, and his deeds. He single-handedly reformed the military chaplaincy, bringing respect and equal opportunity to the offices of Full Gospel chaplains.

Jim was a military and spiritual warrior, fighting for the right, opposing the foe, not taking a back seat to the injustices, biases, prejudices, back-handedness that is prevalent in the military chaplaincy. He gave respect to the terms "Full Gospel" and "Pentecostal" in the military chaplaincy. He caused the Department of Defense to realize the need for a greater presence of Full Gospel chaplains at every echelon in the military and to make room for equal representation for chaplains of all religious traditions.

Jim Ammerman said to Jim Linzey at the conclusion of this recorded interview, "I'm glad you're doing this. And by the way, when you get it in print, send it to the office address, will you, and they'll pick it up for me." Colonel Ammerman wanted it recorded to preserve his message and protect its authenticity in the aftermath of releasing it to the public. For there are always naysayers, from the least expected corners of even Christendom, who have always attempted to undermine the Colonel's message and thwart his stated goals. Jim Linzey facilitated the Colonel's desire to speak for himself and get his message out on his life and his calling.

I knew Jim Ammerman. He has blessed my life in more ways than he could have possibly imagined. And I pray that this book will be an everlasting tribute to such a highly effective and humble servant of the Most High.

Gordon J. Klingenschmitt, Ph.D.
May 2012

Recommended Reading

Ammerman, Charlene and Jim. *After the Storm*. Nashville, TN: Star Song Communications, 1991.

Ammerman, Charlene. *Black Satin Bloomers*. Duncanville, TX: Chaplaincy of Full Gospel Churches, 2002.

Ammerman, Jim. *Supernatural Events in the Life of an Ordinary Man*. Everett, WA, 1996.

Linzey, Verna M. *The Baptism with the Holy Spirit*. Maitland, FL: Xulon Press, 2004

Military Chaplains. *The Leader's Bible*.

Prayers of the United States Armed Forces

A Prayer for the United States Air Force

Heavenly Father, Lord and Savior of us all, we come before You beseeching Your Divine protection over the Air Force as we embark upon our missions. We honor You as our Guide and Comforter as You lead us by Your Spirit day by day. Enable us, Lord, to use the skills and knowledge we have been trained to use to fulfill the charges our rank or station requires of us. Continue to give guidance and wisdom to our Airmen in the fulfillment of the orders and duties they have sworn to carry out. We thank you for your mantle of love over our families whom we trust to your care and guidance that they may live in safety, health, and peace. Protect them from the enemy of our souls as You sustain them with Your love. Strengthen all of us by Your Holy Spirit in all that we do in service to America and the United States Air Force as we are careful to give you the praise, the glory, and our devotion in humble obedience to Your commands as you sustain us by Your blessed Spirit. In Christ Jesus' name we pray. Amen.

– Chaplain, Lieutenant Colonel Jack J. Chinn, USAF (Ret.)

A Prayer for the United States Army

Almighty God, we earnestly ask that, out of your loving and tender mercies, you would place within the minds of your Soldiers the knowledge to do your will in times of war and in times of peace. Graciously impart to your Soldiers the wisdom to discern your will, O Lord, and the moral courage to implement your will in their daily lives. Lead your Soldiers to call upon you so that by your power they may advance from victory to victory, crushing the oppression of wickedness that would otherwise defeat them. And we ask that you would use the Army as one of your righteous tools to establish your justice throughout the world. Amen.

– Chaplain (MAJOR) James F. Linzey, ARNG (Ret.)

A Prayer for the United States Coast Guard

Almighty God, Maker of heaven and earth, by Your will are set the boundaries of the nations. Grant to the men and women who guard our shores that selfless devotion that is woven into the very fabric of Coast Guard tradition. Give to them the skill, wisdom and seamanship that will enable them to thwart every attempt to flood our coasts with contraband, illegal drugs or evil terrorists. In lonely nights as they stand watch, sustain them with your presence. Protect them, O Lord, as they risk their lives to save the lives of others. And when they have weathered life's last storm may they find safe haven in the love of Him who calmed the raging sea and gave His life to save all who trust Him. Through Jesus Christ our Lord we pray. Amen.

– *Commander R. Glen Brown, CHC, USN, (Ret.)*

A Prayer for the United States Marine Corps

Heavenly Father, we lift to you the men and women of the Marine Corps; hold them in your loving hands, protecting them as they protect us. Keep their bodies in your care; keep their hearts true to the ideals of the Corps and the precepts of your Word; keep their minds clear and focused on the task at hand. Reveal your presence and love to them in every situation in life. When at leisure, may they wish to please you; when in harm's way, let them sense your guidance; when wounded or afraid, let them know your comfort; when showing kindness to those in need or to children, may they do it in the knowledge of your approval; and be their Savior to the end of their life and beyond. God bless and protect the Corps as she serves the United States of America. May her cause ever be righteous, and may it be pursued with a true and gallant heart. In the name of Jesus Christ our Lord we pray. Amen.

– Captain Marvin E. Snyder, CHC, USN (Ret.)

A Prayer for The United States Navy

O Lord, our Lord, how great is Your glory throughout all the earth! We call upon our souls, and all that is within us, to praise and bless Your Name. For Your majesty is reflected in all creation. In Your hands are the depth of the sea and the awesome powers of the air. With the eye of faith we observe Your Presence all about us. We thank You, Lord, for the privilege and challenge of serving in the Naval forces of our country; to be the protector, defender, and promoter of the interests and wellbeing of our land. May our mission and purpose serve to promote peace and justice in a world so needful of both. May we fulfill our calling with honor and loyalty, so that Your will may be done on earth through us. For all who sail the oceans and ply its depths and fly its spaces we earnestly seek Your grace and care. May we not fear, for You are our help and our salvation. May we not fail, for You are the strength of our lives. May we not lose courage, knowing that the Eternal God is our refuge and underneath are His everlasting arms. In the Name above all names we pray. Amen.

– *Captain Derke P. Bergsma, CHC, USN, (Ret.)*

A Deployment Prayer

Almighty God, we turn our thoughts to Thee as we make ready to deploy for distant places. Thou knowest the future and will defend us from all adversities both to the soul and body if we will fully trust in Thee. Enable each of us to cheerfully accept his respective place of duty within this unit that we may pass all our days in devotion to our sacred tasks. Watch over our wives, children, and loved ones at home through all the days of our separation, that our return may be a blessed homecoming. Grant us a good spirit, a happy voyage, and a safe return. In Christ's name we pray. Amen.

– Captain Stanford E. Linzey, Jr., CHC, USN (Ret.)

A Prayer for Veterans

From deep within the American heart comes a burning love of country. Out of that love is born service, a service that may be as minimal as passing loyalty to service that demands the willful giving of one's life. The root of that service is the totality of love….a love that weeps when taps are played, a love that snaps to attention when the flag goes by, a love that reaches a hand to a heart-broken Mother, a love that envelopes a Wounded Warrior, a love that places distinctive honor on men and women who have accepted the call to Active or Reserve service. Grant that the Veterans of our Armed Forces may be brave in battle, high-hearted in hardships, dauntless in defeat, and gentle in victory. Remember our Veterans, for they have trained themselves in peace to help their country in war; and give them skill and courage, endurance and self-control, in the work now set before them. We commend to thy keeping all those who are venturing their lives on our behalf, that whether by life or by death they may win for the whole world the fruits of their sacrifice and a holy peace. Look in thy mercy, Lord, on those who are called to tasks of special peril in the air or beneath the sea. Even there shall thy hand lead them and thy right hand shall hold them. Help them to do their duty with prudence and with fearlessness, confident that in life or in death, thou, Eternal God, art their refuge and underneath are thy everlasting arms. Amen.

– Captain Stanley D. Miller, CHC, USN (Ret.)

The Commander's Prayer

Eternal Father, strong to save, whose love never faileth, and whose power is over all, I pray now for those under my command. Defend them from peril, grant them strength and courage in adversity, and enable them to always stand tall, proud, and unbowed. Make me ever mindful of those entrusted to my leadership. May I use the best parts of myself to fulfill my responsibilities to them. Make me steadfast in virtue, stainless in example, and ever guided by the will of Him to whom I pray. Amen.

– Captain David W. Plank, CHC, USN (Ret.)

THE LEADER'S PRAYER
THE LEADER'S TRAINING COURSE
UNITED STATES ARMY CADET COMMAND

Almighty and most merciful Father, in whom is the fullness of light and liberty, instill within my heart the passion to lead your people to victory. Inspire me to seek deeper levels of understanding. Enlighten my mind by your Spirit, and be gracious unto me. Grant me the wisdom to know your ways and sound judgment to determine what is best for those I lead. Gracious Father, place within me the sense of duty to you and to America. In all my endeavors, renew my mind, spirit and strength, keeping me safe from all danger, while I give you thanks for all success. Amen!

– Chaplain (MAJOR) James F. Linzey, ARNG (Ret.)
The Leader's Training Course
U.S. Army Cadet Command
Fort Knox, Kentucky
2006

The Sinner's Prayer

Dear heavenly Father, I confess that I am a sinner in need of a Savior. I have been living in sin without You. Without You, my life is empty and depraved. I have followed the sins of my youth, and the sins of my own thinking and actions. I have cared more about myself than of You and others. I believe Jesus Christ is Your only begotten Son. I believe He is God, who came in the flesh. I believe He rose from the dead and in Him, only, is eternal life granted. I earnestly implore you to save me from my sins. Please forgive me for sinning against You, against others, and against my own conscience. Strengthen me to live a holy life. Search my heart, O God. Cleanse my heart from every evil desire. Create in me a clean heart. Renew my spirit. Let me thirst no more. But give me the longing to fulfill Your will and hunger after only righteousness. Lead me to live according to the Scriptures. When I fall, pick me up. Keep me in Your will. Now, fill me with the Holy Spirit. In Jesus' name, I pray. Amen.

Hymns of the United States Armed Forces

The United States Navy Hymn

Eternal Father, strong to save,
Whose arm hath bound the restless wave,
Who bidd'st the mighty ocean deep
Its own appointed limits keep;
Oh, hear us when we cry to Thee,
For those in peril on the sea!

O Christ! Whose voice the waters heard
And hushed their raging at Thy word,
Who walked'st on the foaming deep,
And calm amidst its rage didst sleep;
Oh, hear us when we cry to Thee,
For those in peril on the sea!

Most Holy Spirit! Who didst brood
Upon the chaos dark and rude,
And bid its angry tumult cease,

And give, for wild confusion, peace;
Oh, hear us when we cry to Thee,
For those in peril on the sea!

O Trinity of love and power!
Our brethren shield in danger's hour;
From rock and tempest, fire and foe,
Protect them whereso'er they go.
Thus evermore shall rise to Thee,
Glad praise from air, and land, and sea!

Words by William Whiting (1860)
Music by Rev. John Bacchus Dykes (1861)

The United States Air Force Hymn

Lord, guard and guide the men who fly
Through the great spaces of the sky;
Be with them traversing the air
In darkening storms or sunshine fair

Thou who dost keep with tender might
The balanced birds in all their flight
Thou of the tempered winds be near
That, having thee, they know no fear

Control their minds with instinct fit
What time, adventuring, they quit
The firm security of land;
Grant steadfast eye and skillful hand

Aloft in solitudes of space,
Uphold them with Thy saving grace.
O God, protect the men who fly
Through lonely ways beneath the sky.
Amen.

Verse One by Mary C.D. Hamilton (1915)

The United States Army Song

First to fight for the right, and to build the Nation's might,
And the caissons go rolling along.
Proud of all we have done, fighting till the battle's won,
And the caissons go rolling along.

Refrain
Then it's Hi! Hi! Hey! The Army's on its way.
Count off the cadence loud and strong (TWO! THREE!)
For where e'er we go, you will always know
That the caissons go rolling along.

Valley Forge, Custer's ranks, San Juan Hill and Patton's tanks,
And the caissons went rolling along
Minute men, from the start, always fighting from the heart,
And the caissons keep rolling along.

(Refrain)

Men in rags, men who froze, still that Army met its foes,
And the caissons went rolling along.
Faith in God, then we're right, and we'll fight with all our might,
As the caissons keep rolling along.

(Refrain)
– First Lieutenant Edmund L. Gruber, USA, 1908

The United States Coast Guard Hymn

Eternal Father, Lord of Hosts
Watch o'er the ones who guard our coasts
Protect them from the raging seas
And give them light and life and peace.
Grant them from thy great throne above
The shield and shelter of thy love.
Amen.

– CWO George H. Jenks, Jr., USCG, 1955

The United States Marine Corps Hymn

From the Halls of Montezuma,
To the shores of Tripoli;
We fight our country's battles
In the air, on land, and sea;
First to fight for right and freedom
And to keep our honour clean;
We are proud to claim the title
Of United States Marines.

Our flag's unfurled to every breeze
From dawn to setting sun;
We have fought in every clime and place
Where we could take a gun;
In the snow of far-off Northern lands
And in sunny tropic scenes;
You will find us always on the job
The United States Marines.

Here's health to you and to our Corps
Which we are proud to serve;
In many a strife we've fought for life
And never lost our nerve;
If the Army and the Navy
Ever look on Heaven's scenes;
They will find the streets are guarded
By United States Marines.

Author Unknown, 19th Century
Music from Gendarmes' Duet from the opera
Geneviève de Brabant
by Jacques Offenbach

The Armed Forces Believers' Creed

I believe in God the Father, the Creator of heaven and earth, and in Jesus Christ, His only begotten Son. He was conceived by the Holy Spirit and born of the Virgin Mary. He suffered under Pontius Pilate, was crucified, dead, and buried. He descended into hell. On the third day He rose from the dead. He ascended into heaven and sits at the right hand of God the Father. He will come to judge the living and the dead. I believe in the Holy Spirit, the holy Christian Church, the communion of saints, the forgiveness of sins, the resurrection of the body, and eternal life through Jesus Christ, our Lord and Savior. Amen.

– *Chaplain (MAJOR) James F. Linzey, ARNG (Ret.)*

CREEDS OF THE UNITED STATES ARMED FORCES

THE AIRMAN'S CREED

I am an American Airman.
I am a warrior.
I have answered my nation's call.

I am an American Airman.
My mission is to fly, fight, and win.
I am faithful to a proud heritage,
A tradition of honor,
And a legacy of valor.

I am an American Airman,
Guardian of freedom and justice,
My nation's sword and shield,
Its sentry and avenger.
I defend my country with my life.

I am an American Airman:
Wingman, leader, warrior.
I will never leave an Airman behind,
I will never falter,

And I will not fail.

The Coast Guardsman's Creed

I am proud to be a United States Coast Guardsman.

I revere that long line of expert seamen who by their devotion to duty and sacrifice of self have made it possible for me to be a member of a service honored and respected, in peace and in war, throughout the world.

I never, by word or deed, will bring reproach upon the fair name of my service, nor permit others to do so unchallenged.

I will cheerfully and willingly obey all lawful orders.

I will always be on time to relieve, and shall endeavor to do more, rather than less, than my share.

I will always be at my station, alert and attending to my duties.

I shall, so far as I am able, bring to my seniors solutions, not problems.

I shall live joyously, but always with due regard for the rights and privileges of others.

I shall endeavor to be a model citizen in the community in which I live.

I shall sell life dearly to an enemy of my country, but give it freely to rescue those in peril.

With God's help, I shall endeavor to be one of His noblest Works...

A UNITED STATES COAST GUARDSMAN.

The Marine's Creed

This is my rifle.
There are many like it, but this one is mine.
My rifle is my best friend. It is my life.
I must master it as I must master my life.
My rifle, without me, is useless.
Without my rifle, I am useless.
I must fire my rifle true.
I must shoot straighter than my enemy who is trying to kill me.
I must shoot him before he shoots me. I WILL…

My rifle and myself know that what counts in this war is not the rounds we fire,
the noise of our burst,
nor the smoke we make.
We know that it is the hits that count. WE WILL HIT….

My rifle is human, even as I, because it is my life.
Thus, I will learn it as a brother.
I will learn its weaknesses, its strength, its parts, its accessories, its sights and its barrel.
I will ever guard it against the ravages of weather and damage as I will ever guard my legs, my arms, my eyes and my heart against damage.
I will keep my rifle clean and ready.
We will become part of each other. WE WILL….

Before God, I swear this creed.
My rifle and myself are the defenders of my country.
We are the masters of our enemy.
We are the saviors of my life.

So be it, until victory is America's and there is no enemy, but peace!

The Sailor's Creed

I am a United States Sailor.

I will support and defend the Constitution of the United States of America and I will obey the orders of those appointed over me.

I represent the fighting spirit of the Navy and those who have gone before me to defend freedom and democracy around the world.

I proudly serve my country's Navy combat team with

Honor, Courage, and Commitment.

I am committed to excellence and the fair treatment of all.

The Soldier's Creed

I am an American Soldier.
I am a Warrior and a member of a team.
I serve the people of the United States and live the Army Values.
I will always place the mission first.
I will never accept defeat.
I will never quit.
I will never leave a fallen comrade.
I am disciplined, physically and mentally tough, trained and proficient in my warrior tasks and drills.
I always maintain my arms, my equipment and myself.
I am an expert and I am a professional.
I stand ready to deploy, engage, and destroy the enemies of the United States of America in close combat.

I am a guardian of freedom and the American way of life.
I am an American Soldier.

Core Values of the United States Armed Forces

US Air Force Core Values

Integrity First
Service Before Self
Excellence In All We Do

US Army Core Values

Loyalty
Duty
Respect
Selfless Service
Honor
Integrity
Personal Courage

US Coast Guard Core Values

Honor
Respect
Devotion to Duty

US Marine Corps Core Values

Honor
Courage
Commitment

US Navy Core Values

Honor
Courage
Commitment

U.S. Military Code of Conduct

I

I am an American, fighting in the forces which guard my country and our way of life. I am prepared to give my life in their defense.

II

I will never surrender of my own free will. If in command, I will never surrender the members of my command while they still have the means to resist.

III

If I am captured I will continue to resist by all means available. I will make every effort to escape and to aid others to escape. I will accept neither parole nor special favors from the enemy.

IV

If I become a prisoner of war, I will keep faith with my fellow prisoners. I will give no information or take part in any action which might be harmful to my comrades. If I am senior, I will take command. If not, I will obey the lawful orders of those appointed over me and will back them up in every way.

V

When questioned, should I become a prisoner of war, I am required to give name, rank, service number, and date of birth. I will evade answering further questions to the utmost of my ability. I will make no oral or written statements disloyal to my country and its allies or harmful to their cause.

VI

I will never forget that I am an American, fighting for freedom, responsible for my actions, and dedicated to the principles which made my country free. I will trust in my God and in the United States of America.

U.S. Military Oaths of Office

Oath of Allegiance for Officers of the Armed Forces

The United States Military Oath of Allegiance is taken by members of the United States Armed Services on commissioning. It differs slightly from that of the oath of enlistment that enlisted members recite when they enter the service.

I, _____, do solemnly swear (or affirm) that I will support and defend the Constitution of the United States against all enemies, foreign and domestic; that I will bear true faith and allegiance to the same; that I take this obligation freely, without any mental reservation or purpose of evasion; and that I will well and faithfully discharge the duties of the office on which I am about to enter. So help me God.

Oath of Enlistment into the Armed Forces

The Oath of Enlistment into the United States Armed Forces is performed upon any person enlisting or re-enlisting for a term of service into any branch of the military.

I, _____, do solemnly swear (or affirm) that I will support and defend the Constitution of the United States against all enemies, foreign and domestic; that I will bear true faith and allegiance to the same; and that I will obey the orders of the President of the United States and the orders of the officers appointed over me, according to regulations and the Uniform Code of Military Justice. So help me God.

The Pledge of Allegiance

I pledge allegiance to the Flag
of the United States of America,
and to the Republic for which it stands:
one Nation under God, indivisible,
With Liberty and Justice for all.

- Final Version Approved by Congress, June 14, 1954

The Covenant and the Code of Ethics for Chaplains of the Armed Forces

The Covenant

Having accepted God's Call to minister to people who serve in the armed forces of our country, I covenant to serve God and these people with God's help; to deepen my obedience to the commandments, to love the Lord our God with all my heart, soul, mind and strength, and to love my neighbor as myself. In affirmation of this commitment, I will abide by the Code Of Ethics for chaplains of the United States Armed Forces, and I will faithfully support its purposes and ideals. As further affirmation of my commitment, I covenant with my colleagues in ministry that we will hold one another accountable for fulfillment of all public actions set forth in our Code of Ethics.

The Code of Ethics

1. I will hold in trust the traditions and practices of my religious body.

2. I will carefully adhere to whatever direction may be conveyed to me by my endorsing body for maintenance of my endorsement.

3. I understand as a chaplain in the United States Armed Forces that I will function in a pluralistic environment with chaplains of other religious bodies to provide for ministry to all military personnel and their families entrusted to my care.

4. I will seek to provide for pastoral care and ministry to persons of religious bodies other than my own within my area of responsibility with the same investment of myself as I give to members of my own religious body. I will work collegially with chaplains of religious bodies other than my own as together we seek to provide as full a ministry as possible to our people. I will respect the beliefs and traditions of my colleagues and those to whom I minister. When conducting services of worship that include persons of other than my religious body, I will draw upon those beliefs, principles, and practices that we have in common.

5. I will, if in a supervisory position, respect the practices and beliefs of each chaplain I supervise and exercise care not to require of them any service or practice that would be in violation of the faith practices of their particular religious body.

6. I will seek to support all colleagues in ministry by building constructive relationships wherever I serve, both with the staff where I work and with colleagues throughout the military environment.

7. I will maintain a disciplined ministry in such ways as keeping hours of prayer and devotion, endeavoring to maintain wholesome family relationships and regularly engaging in educational and recreational activities for professional and personal development. I will seek to maintain good health habits.

8. I will recognize that my obligation is to provide for the free exercise of religion for ministry to all members of the military services, their families and other authorized personnel. When on active duty, I will only accept added responsibility in civilian ministry if it does not interfere with the overall effectiveness of my primary military ministry.

9. I will defend my colleagues against unfair discrimination on the basis of gender, race, religion or national origin.

10. I will hold in confidence any privileged communication received by me during the conduct of my ministry. I will not disclose confidential communications in private or in public.

11. I will not proselytize from other religious bodies, but I retain the right to evangelize those who are not affiliated.

12. I will show personal love for God in my life and ministry, as I strive together with my colleagues to preserve the dignity, maintain the discipline and promote the integrity of the profession to which we have been called.

13. I recognize the special power afforded me by my ministerial office. I will never use that power in ways that violate the personhood of another human being, religiously, emotionally or sexually. I will use my pastoral office only for that which is best for the persons under my ministry.

The Role of Military Chaplains

The military is about training lean, mean fighting machines, but military men and women have their weaknesses. Due to the pressures they've been under, military men and women often forget about discipline during rest and relaxation, and they often do things they regret, leaving indelible scars on their consciences. Airmen, coast guardsmen, marines, sailors, and soldiers have to learn to shore up their moral weaknesses. Military chaplains are there to help strengthen these areas of weakness, to make troops spiritually strong.

The military chaplains are there to strengthen the men and women so that they do not find themselves sitting in the infirmary wondering what happened to them. With the help of the Holy Spirit, military chaplains provide hope in the military community so that military men and women don't need to cling to binges to survive life.

Suicide sometimes occurs in the military and presents another danger military chaplains fight. When young military men and women take their lives, it is too late to intervene. Military chaplains provide the Word of God to give uniformed men and women hope. The Gospel is the power of God unto salvation, now and eternally.

Even atheists rely on chaplains for their therapeutic value. There is something present beyond the natural when military chaplains are involved. Furthermore, chaplains provide privileged communication and confidentiality to all military men and women and their families. This provides essential reinforcement. The men and women in the military are put under extreme pressure, taking other's lives and seeing their buddies blown apart. They fight to protect their country and families and everything they hold dear, and they might even save their own lives in the process. Having a chaplain there to share their burden can make all the difference.

There is another aspect to this as well. The goal in each battle is to come back whole, but this goal is not always attained. In such cases, having had a military chaplain to share the plan of salvation might have made an eternal world of difference.

Military men and women need hope so that when they walk onto the battlefield they'll walk back from the battlefield. These are your sons and daughters and your brothers and sisters. Handing out Bibles is a crucial role of military chaplains. But going beyond that and ministering to military men and women from the Bible provides a unified effort to shore up the moral fibre of the military and save lives.

– Chaplain (MAJOR) James F. Linzey, ARNG (Ret.)

THE MEANING OF MARRIAGE

Many people treat the institution of marriage irreverently and enter into it unadvisedly with no fear of God, as if it were "easy come, easy go." This treatment of one of humankind's most serious institutions is one of the reasons why the divorce rate is so high, causing untold emotional anguish and many children to grow up with single or no parents. There are some things about marriage which are best described by not only Jesus' words as shown below, but also by the wedding vows of the historical and authoritative "Form of Solemnization of Matrimony from the 1662 Book of Common Prayer of the Church of England." It eloquently states that marriage is to be entered into "reverently, discreetly, advisedly, soberly, and in the fear of God; duly considering the causes for which Matrimony was ordained."

The three purposes it gives for marrying are as follows: "First, it was ordained for the procreation of children, to be brought up in the fear and nurture of the Lord, and to the praise of his holy Name. Secondly, it was ordained for a remedy against sin, and to avoid fornication; that such persons as have not the gift of continency might marry, and keep themselves undefiled members of Christ's body. Thirdly, it was ordained for the mutual society, help, and comfort, that the one ought to have of the other, both in prosperity and adversity." These are truths espoused by the Church. With society's emphasis on continuing compatibility as the guiding factor for marriage and divorce, it is little wonder that the divorce rate is so high among those who are not committed to the teaching of the Church and to the laws of God. The teachings of the Church are intended for the strong establishment of society, the family unit being the cornerstone.

The teachings of the Church are an elaboration of the laws that Jesus gave when He said, "But from the beginning of the creation, God 'made them male and female.' 'For this cause shall a man leave his father and mother, and cleave to his wife, and the two shall be one flesh.' So then they are no longer two, but one flesh" (Mark 10:6-8, MEV). Jesus' teaching emphasizes the unity between a man and his wife. Jesus also said, "What therefore God has joined together, let not man put asunder" (Mark 10:9, MEV). Based on Jesus' statement, it is a moral obligation to remain married once the marriage is consummated.

There is an exception to the law: adultery on the part of the offending spouse. Jesus makes this clear when He said, "But I say to you that whoever divorces his wife, except for marital unfaithfulness, causes her to commit adultery. And whoever marries her who is divorced commits adultery" (Matthew 5:32, MEV). This is the sole exception given. No comment on emotion or desire is added. Feelings come and go, but commitment is commanded by God and pledged by the couple when making the marital vows. The Scriptures reveal that judgment will come upon those who break this vow when the writer of Hebrews states, "Marriage is to be honored among everyone, and the bed undefiled. But God will judge the sexually immoral and adulterers" (Hebrews 13:4, MEV). Breaking a marriage vow is immoral and can cause separation or divorce, will cause misery and guilt, and will bring the judgment of God until or unless repentance or reconciliation and reunification occur. Sometimes, sadly, one partner chooses adultery and opts to depart. If your spouse leaves against your wishes, your spouse cannot take your joy with him or her. Hang on to it, for it will see you through the painful separation. The joy of the Lord is your strength.

However, instead of leaving, the offending spouse may repent, and repentance can avert the judgment of God, and it can save a marriage. Choosing repentance and reconciliation in the face of adultery is commendable, respectable, honorable, and rewarded by God. Adultery is given as a permitted cause of divorce; this does not mean the couple *must* separate, only that they *can*.

Here is where military chaplains are relevant. The military leans heavily on chaplains to help military couples remain together, and a chaplain can provide counseling and prayer for the couple. Military couples are advised to receive the vital assistance they offer. By all means, take advantage of it. Really, they are there to help. This sort of outside intervention can help put a shattered marriage back together, aiding the couple in identifying areas of weakness and trouble and assisting them in resolving the difficulties. Counseling is also available before marriage and can aid in keeping a stable marriage strong and successful.

However, ultimately it is your choice. Outside help can only go so far: The burden of success ultimately rests on the couple, not on the chaplain. Couples decided they would succeed at their marriage when vowing before God and before witnesses during the wedding ceremony to remain married "until death us do part." The couple must then make the daily choice to honor the vows they made before God or face judgment. If your marriage is faltering, trust God, and see what He will do for you today.

There is a man who is respected by the Orthodox Church, the Roman Catholic Church, all the Protestant churches, and even by religious leaders of all religions. His name is Rev. Dr. Billy Graham. Here is a highly reputable leader whose marriage withstood the test of time because it was built on God's Word. Rev. Graham's marriage was never troubled by speculation or rumors or divorce, and he is respected for it as a leader of leaders. When a man and a woman follow God's leadership as did Rev. and Mrs. Graham, their marriage will remain intact, because God does not lead people into division. He leads people in the way of forgiveness and peace, and gentleness and love, the way marriages thrive. Paul the Apostle said, "Let all bitterness, wrath, anger, outbursts, and blasphemies, with all malice, be taken away from you. And be kind one to another, tender-hearted, forgiving one another, just as God in Christ also forgave you" (Eph. 4:31-32, MEV). This kind of forgiveness and care serves to cement a union.

The best state of all is an intact marriage. When a man and his wife choose joy over sadness and union over divorce, the Holy Spirit will be the lifelong bond between the two.

– Chaplain (MAJOR) James F. Linzey, ARNG (Ret.)

The Ten Commandments as The Foundation of America

There is, lately, a dispute over whether or not the Ten Commandments should be left hanging in courtrooms, schools, or any public place. Those who would deny them a place argue that they are solely religious in value and have no place in the secular state.

This argument ignores the historical role the Ten Commandments have played in our nation's history. In fact, a look at the original documents of our Founding Fathers demonstrates that the Founding Fathers deliberately worked from the premise of the morality of the Holy Bible, especially from the Ten Commandments. Keeping the Ten Commandments on public display is not, then, a recent attempt by Christians to take over the founding documents or to intrude themselves on public life.

The dispute over the nature of the Commandments also arises because of an ambiguity in the phrase "moral values." People often assume that morality and moral values are religious in nature and thus should be kept out of the political and legal arena. It is true that many religions use morality as an important part of their beliefs, but the term itself, and the conduct depicting morality, is not religious. A closer tie would be ethics, a set of internalized and carefully chosen beliefs. Even "spiritual values" are not necessarily religious, for "spiritual" is most often contrasted with material, physical, or corporeal. In fact *Webster's Dictionary* defines spiritual as "of or pertaining to the spirit or soul, as distinguished from the physical nature." It defines spirit as the "the principle of conscious life; the vital principle in humans, animating the body or mediating between body and soul." These definitions suggest the dual nature of humankind—spiritual and material. A human being functions through both the physical body and also through the intellect and will. Morality, then, often associated with the spiritual part of man rather than the physical, refers to actions based on the question of right and wrong, a choice of behavior and of a basis for behavior.

People mistakenly think that the Ten Commandments are only about religion or worshipping God and that, as a consequence, they can, or even should, be shunted aside and removed from the public forum. Taking this view ignores the fact that, as a set of rules, they are solid and valuable. They talk of God, but they are also about living a decent moral life in community with other people. They are about being human and treating others as human beings. They have to do with every person's relationship to every other person, and leaders looking for the foundation to moral living need to pay attention to them.

The Ten Commandments as given in the twentieth chapter of Exodus can be abbreviated to these:

> You shall have no god before Me
> (the Judeo-Christian Lord God).
>
> You shall not make idols in any form or
> worship idols in any form.
>
> You shall not misuse the name of the Lord
> (in swearing or false prophesying).
>
> You shall keep the Sabbath day holy.
>
> You shall honor your father and mother.
>
> You shall not murder.
>
> You shall not commit adultery.
>
> You shall not steal.
>
> You shall not lie.
>
> You shall not covet anything that belongs to anyone else.

Notice that three of these commandments refer directly to God himself. The First and Third talk of worshipping him and regarding him with respect. The Second is about worship and also about priorities (more on that later). In the main, these Ten Commandments are statements of the way to act if we would be moral people. They are guidelines for treating one another well and reasonably.

We cannot violate these standards of behavior in our relationships to those around us and still call ourselves moral beings. They describe common good behavior for both leaders and followers. We live in community with other human beings, and for the community to survive, certain rules or laws must be in effect. These ten "rules" (or "commandments" for living in community) that God gives are the basic core of community survival. We don't, unfortunately, always choose to follow these rules. It is much easier to lie sometimes than to be the moral person who tells the truth, and we often choose the easy way. Society wants to blame our moral failures on our inability to keep such stringent demands from a stern God. However, notice that God asks nothing in the seven social commandments that we have not asked of others, often at much greater length, in legal codes.

At one level, these are simple commands, a matter of treating one another well, a matter of action. There is another way of looking at these commandments, though, seeing the moral undergirding to them, and this, also is valuable. In the New Testament, the part of the Bible that tells of Christianity and life after Jesus came to earth, we are told how to transfer the commandments of action given in the Old Testament to commandments of attitude. Moral beings live more by attitude than by actions, although attitudes precede actions. It is relatively easy for actions to measure up to some sort of code of behavior while the mind and heart are bitter, resentful, angry, hateful, and feeling just the opposite of what the bodily actions indicate. In other words, we can politely say, "I'm sorry" when we are coerced to do so by our parents or teachers, while at the same time hatefully saying in our hearts, "I'm glad I kicked your face in."

Jesus deals with this discrepancy between action and attitudes in his teachings on the Ten Commandments. In the fifth chapter of Matthew Jesus refocuses the Sixth Commandment from the action of murder to the attitude of murder; "You have heard that it was said by the ancients, 'You shall not murder,' and whoever murders shall be in danger of the judgment. But I say to you that whoever is angry with his brother without a cause will be in danger of the judgment; and whoever says to his brother, 'Raca,' will be in danger of the council of the Sanhedrin. But whoever says, 'You fool,' will be in danger of fire of hell" (Matt. 5:21-22). Murder is no longer simply a physical act but a moral one. It is not just the action of killing someone, but it is the attitude of being angry with our brothers and neighbors. Likewise, Jesus tells us that "whoever looks on a woman to lust after her has committed adultery with her already in his heart" (Matt. 5:28). Adultery is not simply taking someone not our spouse (an action), but it is looking at someone lustfully (an attitude) whether we take that person or not.

People are right when they complain that moral living is hard. It is not based simply on the physical keeping of the law or the Ten Commandments of the Old Testament, but it is keeping the intent of the law in our hearts and minds. It is the willingness to live according to the moral context behind the laws rather than trying to get around or avoid their meaning. The Ten Commandments ask us to do that. Yet, difficult or not, we can readily see that whether we are speaking of the actions or the attitudes, living in community requires that we follow basic commands of getting along with others and valuing the lives of others.

Why, then, is it so difficult for people to accept by the Ten Commandments? Most of us would agree that we don't want others to lie, cheat, kill, commit adultery with our spouses, or covet our possessions. Why don't we keep the commands ourselves if we want others to do so? The basic problem is with people's choice of object of worship. The first commandment tells us to put God first, and if we truly love the Lord God first—put no other gods or possessions or people before Him—then we have help in keeping the rest of the commands, but many people have chosen not to follow the First Commandment, often denying it all together. People like to put themselves first, or put their jobs or careers or possessions or money or fame or health first. Those things or people who are most important to us are the ones who become our "gods" or "idols" (as mentioned in the Second Commandment). If we don't put God first, we have weakened the reasons to follow the rest of the commandments. Without a moral reason, we lose track of the social reason, and if it suits us to lie or violate any of the other nine commandments, we do so. Once we break one commandment, it is easier to break all the rest of them. We may not actually physically kill a person, but we will allow ourselves to hate someone to the extent that we almost wish that person dead, a wish that corrodes our relationships with others.

We also have difficulty in following the Ten Commandments because of the woeful example set by our leaders. Because the leaders of our nation have not kept the code of morality alive in their dealings with the American people, the people of our nation in turn do not keep moral conduct. Our leaders break the Ten Commandments every day in the political life, the social life, the physical life of our nation. The people of our nation know the leaders lie and cheat, so the people see no reason they should not follow suit. If the big leaders get away with it, why shouldn't the small everyday people also get away with it? So the moral code goes out with the garbage and the morality of the nation degenerates to selfishness and trying to get away with more than the other guy gets away with.

America needs the Ten Commandments, and she needs people who follow them. Leaders, in particular, are called to set an example for their followers. The Ten Commandments, in act and thought, form the basis for such a model.

– Chaplain (MAJOR) James F. Linzey, ARNG (Ret.)

King Solomon Refutes Communism

"My son,

if sinners entice thee, consent thou not.

If they say, Come with us, let us lay wait for blood,

let us lurk privily for the innocent without cause:

Let us swallow them up alive as the grave;

and whole, as those that go down into the pit:

We shall find all precious substance,

we shall fill our houses with spoil:

Cast in thy lot among us;

let us all have one purse:

My son,

walk not thou in the way with them;

refrain thy foot from their path:

For their feet run to evil,

and make haste to shed blood.

Surely in vain the net is spread in the sight of any bird.

And they lay wait for their *own* blood;

they lurk privily for their *own* lives.

So *are* the ways of every one that is greedy of gain;

which taketh away the life of the owners thereof."

– King Solomon
Proverbs 1:10-19, KJV

LEADERSHIP QUOTES ON RELIGIOUS FREEDOM

"The highest story of the American Revolution is this: It connected in one indissoluble bond the principles of civil government with the principles of Christianity."

–John Adams, former United States President

"The highest glory of the American Revolution was this: it connected in one indissoluble bond the principles of civil government with the principles of Christianity."

–John Quincy Adams, former United States President

"I conceive we cannot better express ourselves than by humbly supplicating the Supreme Ruler of the world…that the confusions that are and have been among the nations may be overruled by the promoting and speedily bringing in the holy and happy period when the kingdoms of our Lord and Saviour Jesus Christ may be everywhere established."

–Samuel Adams, a United States Founding Father

"We have grasped the mystery of the atom and rejected the Sermon on the Mount ... The world has achieved brilliance without wisdom, power without conscience. Ours is a world of nuclear giants and ethical infants."

–General Omar Bradley, United States Army (Ret.)

"The American nation from its first settlement at Jamestown to this hour is based upon and permeated by the principles of the Bible."

–David Joseph Brewer, former Supreme Court Justice

"The Lord our God be with us, as He was with our fathers; may He not leave us or forsake us; so that He may incline our hearts to Him, to walk in all His ways…that all peoples of the earth may know that the Lord is God; there is no other."

–George H.W. Bush, former United States President

"They [the American Founding Fathers] were intent upon establishing a Christian commonwealth in accordance with the principle of self-government. They were an inspired body of men. It has been said that God sifted the nations that He might send choice grain into the wilderness. . . . Who can fail to see it in the hand of Destiny? Who can doubt that it has been guided by a Divine Providence?"

–Calvin Coolidge, former United States President

"The real fire within the builders of America was faith – faith in a provident God whose hand supported and guided them…"

–Dwight D. Eisenhower, former United States President

"Congress shall make no law respecting an establishment of religion, or prohibiting the free exercise thereof."

–First Amendment to the Bill of Rights

"The [U.S.] Constitution is the bedrock of all of our freedoms. Guard and cherish it, keep honor and order in your own house, and the Republic will endure."

–Gerald R. Ford, former United States President

"God governs in the affairs of man. And if a sparrow cannot fall to the ground without His notice, is it probable that an empire can rise without His aid?"

–Benjamin Franklin, a United States Founding Father

"The next time a friend or colleague says that religious expression has no place in the public square and that discussion of God has no place in our children's history and government classes, you will only need to tell them . . . of God's role in America's history – and America's future."

–Newt Gingrich, former Speaker of the House of Representatives

"The sacred rights of mankind are not to be rummaged for, among old parchments, or musty records. They are written, as with a sun beam, in the whole volume of human nature, by the hand of the Divinity itself; and can never be erased or obscured by mortal power."

–Alexander Hamilton, former United States President

"We think it is incumbent upon this people to humble themselves before God on account of their sins...[And] also to implore the Divine Blessing upon us, that by the assistance of His grace, we may be enabled to reform whatever is amiss among us, that so God may be pleased to continue to us the blessings we enjoy."

–John Hancock, American Revolutionist

"There is a just God who presides over the destinies of nations..."

–Patrick Henry, a United States Founding Father

"That Book, sir, is the rock on which our Republic rests."

–Andrew Jackson, former United States President

"Providence has given to our people the choice of their rulers, and it is the duty, as well as the privilege and interest of our Christian nation to select and prefer Christians for their rulers."

–John Jay, First Chief Justice of the United States Supreme Court

"God who gave us life gave us liberty. And can the liberties of a nation be thought secure when we have removed their only firm basis, a conviction in the minds of the people that these liberties are a gift from God? That they are not to be violated but with his wrath? Indeed I tremble for my country when I reflect that God is just, and that His justice cannot sleep forever."

–Thomas Jefferson, former United States President

"The rights of man come not from the generosity of the state but from the hand of God.."

–John F. Kennedy, former United States President

"The heavens declare the Glory of God and the firmament showeth his handiwork."

–King David (Psalm 19:1, KJV)

"It is my constant anxiety and prayer that I and this nation should be on the Lord's side."

–Abraham Lincoln, former United States President

"We have staked the whole future of American civilization, not upon the power of government, far from it. We have staked the future of all our political institutions upon the capacity of mankind for self-government; upon the capacity of each and all of us to govern ourselves, to control ourselves, to sustain ourselves according to the Ten Commandments of God."

–James Madison, former United States President

"...whereby our said people, inhabitants there, may be so religiously, peaceably, and civilly governed, as their good life and orderly conversation may win and incite the natives of this country to the knowledge and obedience of the only true God and Saviour of mankind and the Christian faith."

–Massachusetts Bay Charter

"In the name of God, Amen. We, whose names are underwritten, the Loyal Subjects of our dread Sovereign Lord, King James, by the Grace of God, of England, France and Ireland, King, Defender of the Faith ... having undertaken for the Glory of God, and Advancement of the Christian Faith, and the Honor of our King and Country, a voyage to plant the first colony in the northern parts of Virginia ..."

–Mayflower Compact, 1620

"Religion, morality, and knowledge, being necessary to good government and the happiness of mankind, schools and the means of education shall forever be encouraged."

–The Northwest Ordinance, an Act of the United States Congress

"The time has come to turn to God and reassert our trust in Him for the healing of America.... Our country is in need of and ready for a spiritual renewal."

–Ronald Reagan, former United States President

"We all can pray. We all should pray. We should ask the fulfillment of God's will. We should ask for courage, wisdom, for the quietness of soul which comes alone to them who place their lives in His hands."

–Harry S. Truman, former United States President

"It is the duty of all nations to acknowledge the providence of Almighty God and to obey His will."

–George Washington, former United States President

"If we abide by the principles taught in the Bible, our country will go on prospering and to prosper; but if we and our prosperity neglect its instructions and authority, no man can tell how sudden a catastrophe may overwhelm us and bury all our glory in profound obscurity. Lastly, our ancestors established their system of government on morality and religious sentiment. Moral habits, they believed, cannot safely be trusted on any other foundation than religious principle, nor any government be secure which is not supported by moral habits."

–Daniel Webster, former United States Secretary of State

"No truth is more evident to my mind than that the Christian religion must be the basis of any government intended to secure the rights and privileges of a free people."

–Noah Webster, Father of American Scholarship and Education

"Remember ever; and always, that your country was founded... by the stern old Puritans who made the deck of the Mayflower an altar of the living God, and whose first act on touching the soil of the new world was to offer on bended knees thanksgiving to Almighty God."

–Henry Wilson, former United States Vice President

"America was born a Christian nation. America was born to exemplify that devotion to the elements of righteousness which are derived from the revelations of the Holy Scripture."

–Woodrow Wilson, former United States President

How General Ralph E. Haines, Jr., USA (CONARC) Received the Baptism with the Holy Spirit

General Ralph E. Haines, Jr., was instrumental and supportive of Chaplain (COL) Jim Ammerman in the founding of Chaplaincy of Full Gospel Churches, and served on the Advisory Board.

Here is what happened in Buffalo, New York, in July 1971, with General Ralph E. Haines, Jr., US Army (CONARC).

Chester (Chet) Wyrich, a Full Gospel Business Men's Fellowship, International business man from Buffalo, New York, organized a small convention at a hotel and somehow obtained General Ralph Haines as the speaker for a Saturday morning Military Prayer Breakfast. Commander Carl Wilgus, USN, had begun military prayer breakfasts in the Bureau of Naval Personnel (BUPERS) Admiral's dining room in 1967; and military prayer breakfasts were catching on.

General Haines was the last CONARC (Continental Army Commander). General George Washington was the first CONARC. General Haines commanded all Army Bases in the Continental USA with over 1,000,000 soldiers. Chet invited me to come along to Buffalo as a sort of aide for General Haines, who arrived by military air on Friday afternoon before he was to speak Saturday morning. When General Haines first stepped off the aircraft, he looked weary and worn, and all I could think was "dead." His face looked wrinkled as a prune.

General Haines was persuaded to have supper with us at the Friday evening meeting, where the Lutheran priest, Harald Bredesen, was to speak. I sat on General Haines' left at the head table. Pat Robertson was present. And instead of speaking, Pastor Bredesen asked us to stand and sing "There's a Sweet Spirit in This Place." As we stood and began to sing, General Haines began to tremble! And I positioned myself to catch him, because I thought he may be having a heart attack and dying. Instead, General Haines' arms shot straight up in the air! Light blazed from his face, knocking over people from their tables! General Haines began to shout in another language, as his face became smooth as a baby's, with light radiating from him!

The whole hotel was stirred all Friday night. When General Haines stood to speak at the Military Prayer Breakfast the next morning, he tore up his previously scripted "dry weather report," and made an astounding statement: "I don't know what Jesus is telling me to do, but whatever it is, I am going to do it!"

General Haines then began to visit every Army Base in America. He would gather all the officers in the Base Chapel, to read to them from the General Orders as first laid down by General George Washington, which state: "The Commanding Officer is responsible for the SPIRITUAL LEADERSHIP [my emphasis] of his soldiers." General Haines stated, "Gentlemen, if you are going to be a spiritual leader, you need a spiritual experience. Now let me tell you about mine." He would then confess his salvation and Baptism in the Holy Spirit! He concluded by adding, "It is better to be a private in the Army of Jesus than to be a general in the Army of America."

Therefore, General Haines began to be denounced throughout America, culminating in Senator Jacob Javits of NY denouncing Haines on the floor of the Senate (and in the pages of the *Washington Post*, *NY Times*, and other papers), and finally General Haines' relief as CONARC under President Nixon. But the testimony of the 98 year old "private in the Army of Jesus Christ" continues to echo through the Army and on the front page of a recent 2010 *Army Times.*

by Colonel Myrl Allinder, USMC-Ret.

Colonel Myrl Allinder received the baptism with the Holy Spirit at the Pentagon in 1968 when Captain Stanford E. Linzey, CHC, USN, (the late husband of Dr. Verna Linzey and father of Chaplain (MAJ) Jim Linzey) laid hands on him.

Editorial Note:

Some time after receiving the baptism with the Holy Spirit, General Haines was believed to have been responsible for Chaplain Jim Ammerman forming Chaplaincy of Full Gospel Churches, to endorse Spirit-filled ministers for the military chaplaincy. Captain Stanford Linzey and his son, Chaplain (MAJOR) Jim Linzey, USAR (Ret.), who was endorsed by Colonel Ammerman, spoke for some of their conventions.

www.ingramcontent.com/pod-product-compliance
Lightning Source LLC
Chambersburg PA
CBHW022106040426
42451CB00007B/142